REMEMBER THY CREATOR

REMEMBER THY CREATOR

G. RICHARD CULP

BAKER BOOK HOUSE
Grand Rapids, Michigan

*To the loving memory
of our departed son, James
who in his brief earthly pilgrimage
was ever a lover of truth*

Contents

Illustrations

Foreword

In this foreword to Dr. Culp's book, in which he thoroughly analyzes the various theories of evolution, I unreservedly wish to state my appreciation. Dr. Culp presents his arguments objectively and with considered fairness. It is to be noted that there is no conflict between science and the Bible. This is strikingly true in the search for truth and of particular relevance in the account of the creation. Of special significance is the clear distinction between philosophical speculation and the irrefutable truth of Bible revelation.

The clarity with which the book is written and the easily understood words and sentence structure recommend it in a special way. The thorough discussion of this intricate scientific subject, easily read and understood, is an unusual accomplishment.

It is no happy accident that proteins and their amino acids are always converted to suit the host consuming them; that the earth's tilt of $22\frac{1}{2}$ degrees is just right to sustain life; that the various plants and animals, while showing similarities, have distinctive differences with no observable changes in prospect; that man is the only one with thinking capacity.

The consideration of the arguments proposed from embryology, astronomy, the fossil record, anthropology, genetics, and the laws of inheritance, the proof of the stability of the species, adds to the interest of the book. They clearly establish the truth of the Genesis account of creation as the act of God.

It is noteworthy that Dr. Culp ably shows the warping effect of the theory of evolution. The teaching of this unscientific philosophical speculation has resulted in a closed-minded dogmatism. As an example, anthropological concepts are being changed to meet sociological trends. It is fashionable to exercise tolerance where there is a threat to theoretical belief, even if it is not based on scientific knowledge.

This carefully documented book shows that theistic evolution is the gateway to spiritual disaster. Both natural and theistic evolution are neither scientific nor scriptural.

A careful study of this book will help the searcher for truth to realize that God's Word is a sure and dependable foundation upon which to build.

Fred S. Brenneman, M.D.
(Formerly medical missionary to India and Tanzania; staff physician-psychiatrist at Philadelphia State Hospital, Philadelphia; chief of psychiatric services at Western State Hospital, Staunton, Virginia; director of public health in American Samoa.)

Preface

Although I was at one time an evolutionist myself, for many years I have had the conviction that the teaching of evolution has been a powerful force in unsettling young people and in destroying their faith in the Word of God, turning them away from the message of redemption through the sacrifice of Christ. Having encountered the teaching repeatedly through my college undergraduate studies, later in my graduate school studies, and finally in my training in osteopathic medicine and surgery, I felt a special burden for other young people who would be facing these same teachings. Because of this concern, I began giving a series of lessons on creation and evolution in the biology courses that I taught in high school and college. As a result of these, I was asked to give them in churches in various states, and occasionally before other groups such as the Inter-Varsity Christian Fellowship and the Rotary Club. Some of these chapters were presented in the *Fellowship Messenger,* and subsequently many readers encouraged me to expand them into a book of this nature. The evidence presented in this volume represents a quest for truth over many years, in academic studies, in firsthand nature study in the field, and in medical sciences.

The first two parts of the book contain fewer quotations than the third because they are intended primarily for the ordinary reader

of Christian literature, who has no special interest in quotations
from scientific literature. As the book progresses and the material
becomes more technical, more extensive documentation is utilized.
In a few instances I have used quotations from nontechnical magazines and newspapers, for example, in reports of scientific assem-
blies, where accuracy could be ascertained.

Several persons have helped in the preparation of this book.
Harold Brenneman of Lancaster, Pennsylvania, did most of the
typing and has added many appreciated words of counsel. Millard
Lind of Associated Mennonite Seminaries provided insights into
the Hebrew text of Genesis. I am indebted to the booklet, *The Eye
As an Optical Instrument* (American Scientific Affiliation), for
the material given on this subject, and to the *World Book Encyclopedia* (Field Enterprises Educational Corporation, Chicago),
for some of the material on the heart. Especially appreciated was
the helpfulness extended by the Field Enterprises Educational Corporation, *The National Geographic Magazine,* The Field Museum
of Natural History in Chicago, and the American Museum of
Natural History in New York City in supplying illustrations. I
have also utilized quotations from many other appreciated sources,
for which proper credit is given in the footnotes.

Hopefully the reader will receive a fraction of the joy and inspiration that I always receive when I contemplate, on the one
hand, the beauty and order of God's handiwork, and, on the other,
the inability of the enemies of God's Word to budge it from its
eternal moorings in the mind of God.

G. Richard Culp, D.O.

Part I

Evidence for Divine Creation

1

The Inanimate World

Man is, by nature, an inquisitive creature. One of the questions that has always been prominent in his mind is that of his origin. From where did he come, and how?

The atheist declares that his origin must be explained entirely on a mechanistic basis, by the chance interaction of originally lifeless molecules to form a primeval protoplasmic mass from which all other life has been derived.

The agnostic asserts that "we just can't know." He claims not to be an atheist, and thus does not need to construct as specific a defense for his view. Yet he is equally dogmatic in his assertion, and is not willing to admit that there is a good possibility that one can know! His final conclusions usually are not far removed from those of the atheist.

The Christian believes the divine account of his origin. He is not ashamed to testify for it, for he expects to be in the minority in all the foremost issues of life. Yet his faith is not necessarily a blind one, but is consistent with scientific truth as well.

All men, of course, claim to be guided by truth. It is at once apparent that truth does not contradict itself, that divine truth and truth as manifested in the natural world around us both stem from the God of all the earth, and that the two must and will agree. Divine truth is clearly set forth in the Holy Scriptures, as revealed in Jesus' own words, "Thy word is truth" (John 17:17). Scientific truth observed in the natural world also must have a carefully defined source. Here we touch a most crucial point in our consideration.

What is scientific truth? Science is "systematized knowledge of any one department of mind or matter; acknowledged truths and laws, especially as demonstrated by induction, experiment, or observation" (*Webster's New School and Office Dictionary*). Induction, of course, must be based on *fact*.

Philosophy is broader and more generalized, and is concerned with "the causes of all phenomena of both mind and matter." However, when it depends primarily on finite human reasoning, it rests on a very shaky foundation. The weakness of the ancient Greeks was their attempt to reason everything out, without subjecting their conclusions to *experimentation*. Therefore their conclusions were often faulty, and many of their theories have since been exploded. The Epicureans and Stoics encountered by Paul at Athens were such philosophers. They "spent their time in nothing else, but either to tell, or to hear some new thing" (Acts 17:21). Such philosophizing, divorced from rigid experimental testing, results not in simplifying and clarifying truth, but in multiplying confusion through the multitudinous theories that develop. The philosophers were not particularly characterized by open-mindedness on spiritual issues. It is noteworthy that "when they heard of the resurrection of the dead, some mocked: and others said, We will hear thee again of this matter" (Acts 17:32).

Let us be careful, at the very outset, to distinguish between true science and philosophy, between fact and theory.

The Atmosphere

We are prone to take the air around us for granted. Because it is transparent, colorless, odorless, and tasteless, we are normally unconscious of it. We refer to vessels which contain only air as "empty." Yet, we can be rudely reminded of its presence by sudden powerful gusts and windstorms of even hurricane power. The air is not a simple substance, but a surprisingly complex mixture of gases, some of which are essential to our very lives.

Oxygen

By far the best known of these gases is oxygen. This element is essential to all living organisms, and its presence in sufficient amounts in the air is one of the prime evidences for a divine design in the atmosphere. Oxygen is essential during every moment of our existence because, by the process of oxidation, energy is released to warm our bodies, provide fuel for muscle contraction, and supply energy for all vital processes in the body. Without this energy your heart would not beat, your lungs would not fill, and you could not even maintain a sitting position to read this page; you would fall limply to one side, and your eyes could not follow the print on the page.

There is 21 percent oxygen and 78 percent nitrogen in the air. If the proportion of oxygen were increased substantially (if, for example, the proportion of oxygen and nitrogen were reversed), we would experience extreme and continual hazards. This can be seen by preparing pure oxygen in the laboratory and burning different substances in it. If we light a small quantity of sulfur in air, the burning element produces so little flame and light that one can scarcely detect it. If, however, it is placed in oxygen, it burns rapidly with a vivid, bright blue flame. In the same way steel wool will take on a dull glow when heated in air, but will burst into an intense, sparkling, white light when thrust into oxygen. Just think how much all oxidative processes would be accelerated in 78 percent oxygen! Fires and explosions would be rampant. Iron implements that rust out in ten years now would be useless in three. Even today, some of our forest fires are almost impossible to control. Even after mustering all available fire fighters and equipment, when the wind is strong, the fire continues until rain quenches it. Fire control would be virtually impossible if the nitrogen and oxygen components in the air were reversed. To prevent explosions, hospitals maintain rigid regulations for their oxygen supplies.

On the other hand, if the percent of oxygen were reduced but slightly, we would begin to notice it. In fact, very much reduction would make it impossible for us to maintain an active life as we know it. Thus the amount is just right, neither excessive nor deficient.

Since so much oxygen is needed, it is again providential that its solubility in water is so low that it is not removed from the air into the vast water reservoirs of the earth. However, this low solubility in water would be a serious disadvantage in the blood (where water is the chief constituent) had not the Creator provided a special substance, hemoglobin, that enables oxygen to be taken up rapidly into the blood stream in the capillaries of the lungs.

Nitrogen

Nitrogen also is essential for life, being the characteristic element in proteins. Proteins are part of the living substance called protoplasm, found in every cell of the human body (and in every living plant and animal). Despite the large percentage of gaseous nitrogen in the air, in this form it is useless to us, either as fertilizer for the soil, or as a component of our bodies. This nitrogen from the air cannot be extracted in our lungs; therefore, we exhale the same amount of nitrogen that we inhale. This is because nitrogen, unlike oxygen, is quite inactive, lazily refusing to combine with diverse elements. This, too, is providential. Otherwise, particularly with the aid of electric storms, nitrogen would combine with oxygen. All of the oxides of nitrogen are poisonous (nitrous oxide, used in anesthesia, being by far the most benign).

The Creator has seen fit to provide lowly soil bacteria as the essential link in the nitrogen cycle of the chain of life. Several species are involved. The first bacteria in the cycle "fix" atmospheric nitrogen in the nodules of the roots of legumes (clover, alfalfa, soybeans). Others convert the nitrogen first into nitrites and then into nitrates. The latter form can be taken into the root hairs of other plants and conveyed to the stems, leaves, and fruits. Here they are converted into proteins, and thus become available sources of essential nitrogen compounds in our food and that of livestock.

An interesting sidelight is that in certain aquatic habitats, such as bogs and swamps, legumes providing this link are not present. Here some of the plants are insectivorous, and thus derive their nitrogen from the bodies of the insects they ensnare. In the pitcher plant, insects are attracted to the specialized hollow leaves. These are tubular and partially filled with liquid. Insects flying in try to climb up the slippery walls, only to find that stiff, smooth hairs like bayonets prevent their passage; so they fall back into the liquid and drown. They are gradually digested by enzymes. In the sundew, insects are attracted to spoon-shaped leaves with long, sticky hairs. As the insect becomes entangled in the sticky substance, the hairs gradually bend over and hold the insect fast until it is digested. Venus's flytrap is the most vicious of all, clapping its tooth-rimmed leaves together with a speed that is unusual in the plant world.

Carbon Dioxide

Carbon dioxide is so little understood by most of us that we consider it a waste gas. But this substance, too, is essential for life. In the manufacture of food in the green leaf of plants, the basic first food produced in photosynthesis is glucose, a simple sugar and hence a carbohydrate. The word *carbohydrate* suggests two of the three necessary elements, carbon and hydrogen. Oxygen is the third. The carbon and part of the oxygen are provided for in carbon dioxide, which serves as one of the basic raw materials in photosynthesis, by which all plant food and, indirectly, animal food are manufactured. Not only does our vital food supply depend on carbon dioxide, but the carbon compounds found in the cloth for our clothing, the wood for the construction of our homes, and the fuel for heating them are all derived from carbon dioxide.

The air around us contains only .04 percent carbon dioxide. How can this minute amount be responsible for the quantities of organic material in the plant and animal substances in our environment? This can be explained by the structure of the plant. On the underside of each leaf are great numbers (250,000 per square inch) of tiny, microscopic pores, shaped like eyes, which are called stomata. At night they close to retain the plant's moisture. During the day they are open wide to let in carbon dioxide and discharge oxygen. Just inside these pores are spongy cells with membranes constantly bathed with moisture. Because carbon dioxide is highly soluble in water, it is taken up very rapidly by these membranes, much as water is taken up by a blotter. Considerable volumes of carbon dioxide may be taken up in a relatively short time.

Gases in Balance

We have mentioned how the Lord has provided these elements in the right amounts, with the necessary physical and chemical attributes. Possibly every bit as remarkable is the fact that one can collect air from anywhere above the earth, whether it be above the arctic tundra or over desert sands or above teeming tropical jungles, and find that the rate of 21 percent oxygen to .04 percent carbon dioxide is maintained. When one considers that animal life is constantly converting oxygen into carbon dioxide, and that plants do the same during the night (but produce an excess of oxygen from carbon dioxide during the day), the constancy of the balance of these gases is a remarkable testimony to not only God's power to create, but also His power to *maintain* His universe. It never gets out of balance, except where man has polluted the air.

Atmospheric Protection

It is generally conceded that for any planet to support life, an atmospheric covering like the air is essential. This acts like a mighty sun helmet, preventing extremes in temperature. Without this absorbing envelope, the earth's surface would become intensely hot during the day, and, due to rapid loss by radiation, extremely cold at night. Further, the atmosphere filters out most of the deadly cosmic rays before they reach the earth.

How true it is that "God himself . . . formed the earth . . . to be inhabited" (Isa. 45:18).

The next time you drink in a breath of fresh air, thank God for the life-giving atmosphere that surrounds our earth!

Water

As the air is vital to our very existence, so also is that wonderfully unique liquid, water. The oceans cover three-fourths of the earth's surface. This vast water supply supports teeming billions of creatures on this planet, making us marvel at the provision the Creator has made for His creation. These huge ocean "reservoirs" provide the tremendous water surfaces needed to evaporate moisture for cloud formations. These clouds then float over the continents and condense as rain to water the thirsty land hundreds of miles inland. As it evaporates again, it completes the water cycle referred to in Isaiah 55:10. Each time water vaporizes, it is purified, and every time it condenses and falls to the earth as water or snow, it waters the vegetation.

Water is an essential component of the protoplasm which fills every living cell, whether it be in plants or animals. Therefore it must be in constant supply. Yet water is so abundant that many generations have used it wastefully before we have seen the need for conserving it.

Water has many uses in the body. It is the nearest to a universal solvent, for more things are soluble in water than in any other liquid. Therefore water is ideal for transporting food, heat, vitamins, and hormones to living cells, and removing wastes from them, all in the dissolved state. It helps cushion the muscle fibers and other tissues from blows. It lubricates the joints; we have sixty joints just in our fingers and toes, and we never need to oil them. Water washes our eyes, cleanses the mucous membranes of the nose and throat (along with dissolved substances), and removes wastes from the body through the kidneys. It enables our bodies to maintain a temperature of 98.6° F, as each cubic centimeter which evaporates from the surface of the body removes 539 calories of heat. It is also one of the raw materials in food production in the green plant.

Water has a moderating effect on our environment. It has the highest "specific heat" of any liquid. That is, it will absorb more heat from the environment than any other liquid before its temperature rises one degree. That is why the winters are warmer and the summers cooler near a large body of water.

Water possesses an attribute shared by few liquids. As it begins to cool in autumn, water contracts and grows more dense like most other substances, the coolest water sinking to the bottom. As it reaches a temperature just 4° C above freezing, unlike the vast majority of other substances, it suddenly expands, becomes lighter, and rises to the surface. This means that, before any body of water freezes, all the water must fall to 4° C above freezing. Not only will it need to cool off much more before freezing than it would otherwise, but it will freeze at the surface rather than at the bottom. This forms a protective surface over the water so that freezing then proceeds at a much slower rate than if the surface were exposed directly to freezing winds. If this were not so, our rivers and lakes would freeze solid, and the aquatic life would be frozen with it. Also, if ice would sink to the bottom, it would thaw out much more slowly; many scientists believe it would not thaw completely in an entire summer!

The Bible speaks of the refreshment received from "cold water to a thirsty soul," and Jesus pronouced a blessing upon us when we give a cup of cold water to a little child in His name.

The next time you lift a glass of pure, sparkling water to your lips, thank God for its wonderful qualities.

The Earth

"The earth is the Lord's, and the fulness thereof" (Ps. 24:1).

The movements of the earth are very important to all of us. As the earth moves through space around the sun, it spins on its axis one complete turn every twenty-four hours. It turns like a huge barbecue spit before the flaming sun, yet maintains a relatively constant temperature through day and night, never heating up too much on one side or cooling off too much on the other.

As the earth moves around the sun, it moves as though its axis could not turn — as a man would move in a circle around a lamp in the center of the room, with his face always bent forward toward the north. His face would be toward the lamp on the south end of the room; his left side, as he neared the east wall, going one-fourth of the way around; his back, at the north end; and then his right side, as he moved backward three-fourths of the way around, toward the west wall. The earth is always tipped $22\frac{1}{2}°$ on its axis (from the vertical) toward the North Star. In our summer, the North Pole tips $22\frac{1}{2}°$ toward the sun on the south side of the circle, and the South Pole tips away from it; in our winter, the South Pole tips inward toward the sun and the North Pole tips away from it on the opposite side of the circle. Midway between, at the spring and fall equinoxes, the poles point neither away from nor toward the sun, but diagonally to their respective sides, so the direct rays strike the equator. Thus on the summer solstice (June 21), the North Pole is tipping toward the sun at an angle of $22\frac{1}{2}°$, so that the direct rays of the sun reach to the Tropic of Cancer, and the warming rays reach far into the north to bring summer to the arctic (while winter comes to the southern hemisphere). On the winter solstice (December 21), the North Pole tips $22\frac{1}{2}°$ away from the sun while the South Pole points toward the sun, so that winter comes to the northern hemisphere, and summer to the southern hemisphere (fig. 1). Without this tilting of the earth's axis, the arctic regions would remain permanently frozen, and the equatorial regions would have no relief from intense heat. Land at the latitude of the state of Oregon would be as it is at the autumn and spring equinoxes (September 21 and March 21), with high winds and cold, wet weather. Few crops could grow under such conditions, and there would be no change of seasons. But in the providence of God, summer stretches northward and southward, even to the arctic and antarctic, so that flowers bud and blossom, fruits hang on the branches, and birds return to nest and rear their young. What a tragedy it would be to immense areas on the globe if summer never came! Few plants would grow, little animal life could be supported, and man's habitat would be restricted to a much smaller area of the earth.

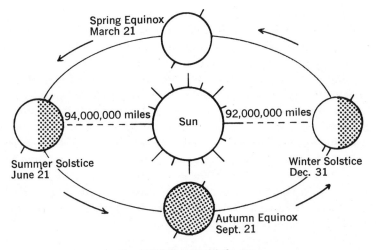

Fig. 1. Rotation around the sun

All of life, and indeed the movements of the air and waters, depend upon a source of energy. It is often said that all energy comes from the sun. This is essentially true. The sun, 92 million miles away, with only a tiny fraction of its radiant energy falling on the surface of our planet, supplies us with all the energy needed by growing plants. Plants produce the food which in turn supplies the energy for us, our domesticated animals, and indeed all animal life. In the rows of countless gardens, in the harvests of grain, hay, and other field crops brought in by toiling farmers of every nation on the globe, in stately forests all around us, this energy is harnessed by the plant and converted into food, fibers, fuel, and lumber that we can use. Yet if we were much closer to the sun, its heat would scorch us, and if we were much farther away, we would freeze to death. For example, if our distance from the sun were reduced by one-half, we would receive not twice as much heat, but four times as much! If it were doubled, we would obtain only one-fourth as much heat. The amount of radiant energy received by a surface from a source of energy is inversely proportional to the *square* of the distance between the two. In addition, this distance must be balanced with the thickness of the atmosphere, the size and intensity of the sun as the source of energy, the rotation of the earth on its axis, and the tilting of the axis. Did it just "happen" that the earth is just the right distance for all these factors to work together for our good and to sustain our lives? Such a conclusion would appear to be straining against the facts.

Dr. Arthur H. Compton, professor of physics at the University of Chicago and recipient of the Nobel prize for physics in 1923 for his brilliant discovery of cosmic rays, made this fitting tribute to the evidence for a divine Creator: "For myself, faith begins with a realization that a supreme intelligence brought the universe into being and created man. It is not difficult for me to have this faith, for it is incontrovertible that where there is a plan there is intelligence — an orderly, unfolding universe testifies to the truth of the most majestic statement ever uttered — 'In the beginning God.' "[1]

Certainly it was not just by chance that the earth is in the very place necessary for it to support life. In His great wisdom God designed it so.

The Solar System

"The heavens declare the glory of God, and the firmament showeth his handiwork" (Ps. 19:1).

In 1776, Titius of Wittenberg, a comparatively unknown astronomer and mathematician, made an arresting discovery. He found that by writing down 0, 3, 6, 12, 24, etc. (doubling the product each time), adding 4 to each number, then dividing by 10, he arrived at the values for the respective distances of the planets from the sun in astronomical units, one unit being the distance of the earth from the sun. J. E. Bode, then director of the Berlin Observatory, recognized the singular importance of this discovery and so popularized it that it became known as Bode's Law. At that time Saturn was the farthest known planet, but when Sir William Herschel discovered Uranus in 1781, its calculated distance fit into the scheme well. There was one gap, however. There should have been a planet between Mars and Jupiter, but none had been found; so a diligent search was made in this region. In 1801, Piazzi in Sicily discovered a tiny planet (planetoid or asteroid) in the proposed orbit. Soon others were found, so that by 1890 more than 300 rough, irregular asteroids (which might well be fragments from one original planet) were found to fill in this gap.

When a slight deviation was discovered in the path of Uranus in 1846, astronomers speculated that a yet unknown object might be exerting a gravitational pull upon it. The necessary position of

---

1. *Chicago Sun,* July 24, 1943.

this unseen body was calculated, and upon learning of it the astronomer Johann Galle almost immediately sighted a "new" planet, Neptune. Only Neptune fails to fit into the scheme of Bode's Law. Pluto, the earth-sized planet discovered in 1930, fits in fairly well. (See fig. 2.)

So close are Bode's calculations that for several generations students of science and astronomy have used this scheme as an easy method to remember the approximate distances of the planets from the sun. The chance of even only the first four coinciding with the law would be very remote. The chance of four, four-digit numbers occurring consecutively (for example, 1960, 1961, 1962, and 1963) would be only one in one hundred million! Surely God's fingerprints can be seen in the orderly arrangement of the planets.

The motions of the heavenly bodies are characterized by regularity and order. So regular are they that a planetarium, the instrument that can be found in the larger astronomical observatories, can predict accurately the motions of the stars and planets, and eclipses of the sun and moon, centuries in advance, and can reveal just where and when they were centuries ago out in space. These all speak for a Designer and Planner whose unerring direction has established their courses in the heavens.

As one watches these lights in the heavens in all their sparkling beauty, tracing their appointed paths in space, the stirring words of Johannes Kepler (1571-1630) seem most appropriate. Kepler was the German astronomer who established the science of planetary motion and laid the groundwork for the study of calculus. At the close of one of his works, he meditated: "It remains only

PLANET	Mercury	Venus	Earth	Mars	Asteroids	Jupiter	Saturn	Uranus	Neptune	Pluto
Bode's Calculation	0	3	6	12	24	48	96	192		384
	4	4	4	4	4	4	4	4	4	4
Theoretical Distance	.4	.7	1.0	1.6	2.8	5.2	10.0	19.6		38.8
Actual Distance	.4	.7	1.0	1.5	3.0	5.2	9.5	19.2	30.1	39.5

Fig. 2. Bode's Law

that I should lift up to heaven my eyes and hands from the table of my pursuits, and humbly and devoutly supplicate the Father of lights. O Thou, who, by the light of nature, dost enkindle in us a desire after light of grace, that by this Thou mayest translate us into the light of glory; I give Thee thanks, O Lord and Creator, that Thou hast gladdened me by Thy creation when I was enraptured by the work of Thy hands."[2]

A very recent testimony in similar vein is given by Frederic H. Giles, Jr., an astronomer and professor of physics at the University of South Carolina: ". . . it certainly cannot be denied that the fact of universal design delivers a telling thrust in the direction of God's existence. There is no doubt that the apostle Paul, a man of great intellect, meant to champion the same thought when he said in Romans (Ch. 1:20, AV) that 'the invisible things of him [God] from the creation of the world are clearly seen, being understood by the things that are made, even his eternal power and Godhead. . . .' Today the God of creation is shown to be much more glorious and awesome: our picture of His universe has exploded in space, time, and content, so that our concept of His power and majesty becomes overwhelming."[3]

Truly, "the heavens declare the glory of God . . ."

---

2. Translated by Charles Singer in *Science, Religion and Reality* (New York, 1925), p. 141. Quoted in *Therefore Stand* by Wilbur M. Smith (New York: W. A. Wilde Co., 1945), p. 300.

3. *Behind the Dim Unknown,* ed. John C. Monsma, (New York: G. P. Putnam's Sons, 1966), p. 152.

2

Animal Instincts

The evidences considered thus far have all been inanimate or nonliving. They are of special value, inasmuch as they cannot be explained away on the basis of organic change and survival of the fittest. On the other hand, some of the most dramatic, and perhaps irrefutable, arguments indicating a divine Creator can be gathered from the instincts observed in the animal kingdom. Let us take a brief look at a few of God's creatures and notice His design in their behavior.

Bird Nests — Who Is the Architect?

If, for example, the eggs of a species of wild bird are taken from the parental nest and artificially incubated, the birds will hatch and grow, and in maturity they will select a mate and build a nest exactly like that of their parents, even though they have never seen one like it. The ruby-throated humming bird will skillfully fashion its nest with plant down, mosses, and lichens, binding on the latter with spider web, the entire structure being about the size of a thimble, but looking deceptively like a bump on a branch. In contrast, the great blue heron will build its nest high in a tall tree overlooking marshy land, using large sticks to construct a nest the size of a wash tub. The Baltimore oriole will use plant fibers and cotton strings to produce a purse-shaped nest suspended from a drooping tree branch, allowing it to sway in the breeze. How detailed these instincts can be is demonstrated by the great crested flycatcher, which will bring to his nest the discarded skin of a blacksnake if one can possibly be found.

Bird Migrations — Who Is the Pilot?

The migrations of birds are also striking. The robin-sized golden plover begins its northward journey from northern Argentina, Uruguay, and southern Brazil as the days grow shorter and autumn is approaching in the southern hemisphere. Its flights are short, allowing for feeding along the way as it works its way northward through Central America toward its summer nesting ground in northern Canada, where spring is approaching. After rearing its young and when the days grow shorter in autumn, it begins its southward journey in short flights to Newfoundland, where it takes off on its now-famous, nonstop flight to South America (although sometimes touching down at Bermuda or the Caribbean Islands).

The Pacific plover's nonstop flight from the Aleutian Islands to Hawaii is a distance of over two thousand miles. How does it find its way to its tiny island destination without chart or sextant? These incredible flights, propelled by the energy from a few ounces of body fat, are themselves marvels of efficiency.

The total journey of the Arctic tern is even longer, extending from the far north above the Arctic Circle to the Antarctic, an annual round trip of 22,000 miles (almost enough to encircle the earth at its greatest dimension). Because it leaves the Arctic just after the sun is beginning to dip below the horizon at midnight, after six months of continuous light, and arrives at the Antarctic about the time the midnight sun can be seen for six months, it spends most of its life in nightless splendor.

Several features about these flights are difficult — some are impossible — to explain from the evolutionary viewpoint. First, these birds begin to leave before the fall frosts, while their food supply is in its greatest abundance. They do not leave because of apparent necessity. Second, they are no longer with their parents who, therefore, cannot guide them on their first long flight. Third, and perhaps most significant of all, they cannot be explained by any theory of adaptation to the environment, so prominent in the evolutionists' arguments.

It is quite apparent that the Arctic tern, which is so fond of cold climates, did not gradually extend its migration from the Arctic to the Antarctic (or vice versa), as the torrid equatorial climate would discourage this extension long before the equator was crossed and more moderate climates were found far on the other side. Indeed, in its flight it must cross the broad region of the equatorial calms, where the air is traveling vertically upward in hot blasts to the upper atmosphere, which would naturally repel any cool-climate inhabitant attempting to gradually extend its range. This argues strongly for an inherited pattern of behavior extending back to the time of creation. In other words, these instincts were acquired by the birds not over a long period of time, but by direct creation. So God left His fingerprints in His creation, and we see them today.

Fish Migrations — Whose Hand Is Guiding?

While our birds are flying south for the winter, the Pacific salmon are swimming from salt water to fresh water to spawn.

Their life cycle begins in pools in the headwaters of the clear streams that pour into the Columbia River and the Pacific Ocean. Here the salmon eggs are hatched, and the tiny fish grow to fingerling size before they begin their journey downstream to its mouth and out into the open sea. During the next three to five years, they feed on shrimp and smaller fish, some swimming northward to Alaska and others southward to California, cruising the Pacific in search of food, which is usually abundant.

When they reach maturity, each fish becomes possessed with an insurmountable urge to return to the same fresh water stream from which it came. This has recently been proven by tagging the fingerlings before they leave fresh water. They now head back to the mouth of the stream and fight their way upward through rapids, leaping over waterfalls up to twelve feet high. When dams are built across the larger streams, fish locks or "ladders" must be constructed around them, or the salmon will try to leap over the huge structures until they die of exhaustion.

I have stood by the banks of the crystal clear, forested streams in Washington state, as the magnificent Chinook salmon come gliding back into their ancestral waters, each flick of their powerful tails bolting them forward like rockets. They are now oblivious to the presence of man as they return, often tattered and bleeding, after their long journey, sometimes for many hundreds of miles over rocks, snags, and waterfalls, in answer to this urge which the Creator of all things has implanted within them and which will not be suppressed. Here they spawn and die, and the wonderful cycle of life begins again in the next generation.

As the salmon are swimming upstream after leaving the ocean, they meet eels coming the other direction toward the sea. These long, slippery fish have a life history that is one of the most intriguing of all. The eastern eels spend most of their lives in the freshwater streams of eastern North America, from Florida to Canada and westward to Michigan. When reaching maturity at five to fifteen years and a length of about three feet, they swim downstream in autumn and out into the ocean where they are found only at spawning time. They are making their way inerrantly toward their spawning ground in the Sargasso Sea, near the Bermuda Islands. Here they are joined by other species from Europe which come to the same place at breeding time.

The Sargasso Sea is a most unusual expanse of ocean water, covering about two million square miles. It derives its name from the unique sargassum weed, which is found only in that area and is unrelated to the seaweed in coastal areas. Here the sargassum weed thrives and reproduces in water two to four miles deep, supported by air sacs which look like tiny grapes. In the days of sailing craft, the thick patches of weeds gave rise to fantastic tales of scores of ghost ships, whose crews reportedly perished of starvation when their vessels became enmeshed in the tangled seaweeds. Although the outer fringes of the water are surrounded by great currents, including the mighty Gulf Stream, the waters within the Sargasso Sea are almost motionless. Furthermore, the water is bluer, saltier, and warmer than the surrounding waters, and it is very clear. A white disc six feet in diameter, lowered 200 feet into the water, could still be clearly seen with the naked eye.

These are the waters to which the American and European eels come to lay their eggs and die. The fertilized eggs develop, and the following spring the young eels are long and ribbon-like, so transparent that one can read a printed page through them. The American eels now head toward the waters from which their parents came. As these tiny creatures begin their year-long journey through a thousand miles of trackless salt water, without chart, compass, or the presence of their parents (which have died), who guides them so accurately back to repopulate their ancestral waters? (See fig. 3.)

As the European eels begin their journey, they face over three thousand miles of ocean before they enter the freshwater streams

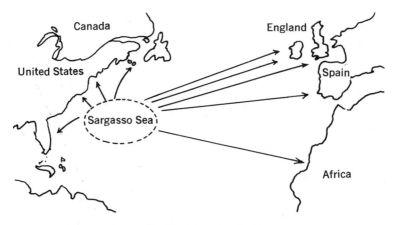

Fig. 3. Migration route of eels

of England, France, and Norway, from which their parents came three years earlier. Furthermore, the American eels never become confused and end up in Europe, nor do the European eels become misled and journey to America! Surely, only an instinct implanted by a divine Creator can guide these tiny creatures aright.

The evolutionist would like to believe that the return of the eels to the sea to spawn is proof that all life comes from the sea. This is disproven by the many species of salmon which return to fresh water at spawning time. Both eel and salmon, by their unerring migrations, show the imprint of the finger of God!

3

Human Organs and Homeostasis

The Eye

If we could retain only one of our five senses, most of us would choose sight. Seeing enables us to continue to draw from the spiritual reservoirs of the Word of God, and to enrich our lives with the knowledge of the fascinating world around us, both past and present. With the eye we see the flaming sunset, the tranquil water of lake and stream, the wildflower that bejewels the forest in the spring. We can judge distance, discern the subtle smile of a beloved friend, and perceive imminent dangers that threaten us. We can manipulate tools to fashion furniture, clothing, and intricate machinery.

Perhaps the most fitting tribute to the efficiency of the eye that has ever been printed is the monograph, *The Eye as an Optical Instrument,* written by Frank Allen, emeritus professor in physics at the University of Manitoba, and published by the American Scientific Affiliation. He establishes that, though the eye is not without defects, these defects are so counterbalanced and compensated for that it was even difficult to discover some of them. Let us consider some of these properties associated with the lens (fig. 4).

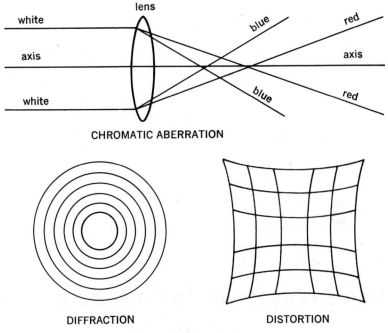

CHROMATIC ABERRATION

DIFFRACTION   **DISTORTION**

Fig. 4. Properties of a lens

Chromatic aberration (the failure of a simple lens to bring light of different colors to the same focus). A glass lens tends to break up "white" light into its constituent wave lengths. The shorter, blue-violet rays are more easily bent (refracted) and focus on the axis of light nearest the lens, whereas the longer red rays are less easily bent and thus cross farthest from the lens, the remaining wave lengths or colors being in between. This phenomenon can often be seen in older glass windows and bottles, where each object seen through the glass seems to have a rainbow border. Significantly, this defect is more in evidence near the *edge* of a lens.

Because 70 percent of the light passing through a 2-mm diameter pupil falls on a retinal area of only 0.005-mm diameter, the aberration is very small. The remaining rays, which are more widely diffused, are therefore unnoticed, so that, as we know from experience, the image is free from colored edges.

Diffraction (bending or spreading light waves). This quality, like chromatic aberration, also is due to the spreading of the waves of light, but the effect is opposite since the spread is greatest with the red rays of light and least with the blue-violet rays. White light is brought to focus as a disc composed of dark and light concentric circles around a bright spot in the center, resembling a rifle target. The central bright spot receives 84 percent of incoming light. Proceeding outward from it, the intensity drops rapidly, the first ring receiving only 1/57 of the total, and the others, correspondingly less. Because of the short focal length (between the lens and the retina) of the eye, however, this effect is small. Further, as it acts in opposition to chromatic aberration, increasing as the latter decreases, for example, these two qualities tend to balance each other and leave the image essentially unchanged. One remarkable use of this phenomenon, however, is in the study of the stars (and similar single points of light), as a ray of light stimulating a single cone (color-sensitive cell) in the retina will transfer the illumination to many surrounding cones, making it possible for us to see the stars which would otherwise never be seen.

Spherical aberration. A biconvex (bulging outward on both surfaces) spherical lens refracts rays near the margin more than those in the center. Thus the marginal focus is nearer the lens than that of the latter and tends to blur the image. This characteristic is virtually eliminated by the lens being immersed in fluid media of nearly the same index of refraction, in contrast with a glass lens in contact with air. Further, this imperfection is proportional to the intensity of light, but as the intensity increases the pupil constricts or narrows, so that spherical aberration is reduced to an insignificant factor.

Distortion. A convex lens tends to produce a distorted image, in which straight lines in the image appear to be bowed. This is compensated for by the retina, which is just concave enough to counterbalance the convexity of the lens.

Let us now consider some of the positive features that put the eye in a place of superiority among optical instruments:

Refraction. The lens is unique among all optical instruments in that it consists of many layers, like those of an onion. The layers vary in their indices of refraction, from 1.386 at the surface to 1.406 at the center. This quality increases the refracting power of the lens, so that it can more easily bend the rays of light entering the eye and focus them on the retina.

Accommodation. By this means the shape of the lens is changed automatically, thinning out for distant objects and thickening for close ones, so that the image of the object, whether near or far, will be clearly and sharply focused on the retina. No other lens has this property. When the lens thins out for focusing on distant objects, the tiny ciliary muscle within the eye relaxes, while the choroid, by virtue of its elasticity, exerts its force to accomplish this effect of thinning. The force of the choroid, however, diminishes steadily during the movement, so that there is no jerk that might prove injurious to the lens. When the lens is thickened at the center for close objects, it does so because of the elastic force of the lens capsule and the contraction of the ciliary muscle working together to achieve this end. The elastic force of the capsule constantly diminishes during this action, again to prevent any sudden and dangerous deformations of the lens. Thus the choroid works antagonistically but smoothly against the action of the capsule and the ciliary muscle.

Mobility. The six external eye muscles attached to the outside of the eyeball are in pairs, the members of each pair working in opposite directions (antagonistically) and thus keeping each eye in its proper place. The coordination manifested by these muscles is nearly perfect; the eyes move back and forth or up and down or diagonally while following a moving object, so that the two images of the eyes always coincide. In the opinion of Helmholz, ". . . it is this rapidity of movement which really constitutes the chief advantage of the eye over other optical instruments."[1] Since his time, however, other outstanding advantages have been demonstrated.

Sensitivity to light. In the *Bulletin of the U.S. Bureau of Standards,* this sensitivity of the retina is expressed in a relative way by stating that it is 300,000 times more sensitive than the best modern radiometer, which can detect the radiation from a candle 52 miles away![2]

The range of light intensity to which the retina is sentitive is almost beyond belief. The intensity of light from a sheet of white paper in the full sun is ten million times that of the intensity outdoors at night. It is *ten billion* times that of the absolute threshold of vision. As Nutting states so well, "In operation over the enormous range of ten billion to one, the eye far exceeds in range any physical instrument."[3] It is able to do this by automatically adjusting the sensitivity of the retina to the brightness of the source

1. Hermann L. F. Von Helmholz, *Handbuch der Physiologischen Optik* (1856-66).
2. Vol. 14 (1918), p. 507.
3. *American Journal of Physiology,* Op. 1 (1920), p. 152.

of light, as the change in pupil size can effect a maximal difference of only ten to one.

One can only meditate in admiration of the Creator at the manner in which the eye, with so many factors in delicate balance, functions almost flawlessly. Well did Sir Isaac Newton ask, "Was the Eye contrived without Skill in Opticks?"

In comparing the great strides made in perfecting optical instruments with the work of the Creator, Frank Allen testifies, "Infinitely greater is the glory of the Divine Designer not only in contriving the far simpler and much more efficient optical system of the eye, but also in establishing biological laws by which the minute details of ocular construction have been transmitted with unimpaired precision to countless individuals of all generations of mankind."[4] How perfectly do our eyes bear witness to the design of the Master Craftsman, the Creator of heaven and earth!

Homeostasis

The term *homeostasis* was coined by Walter B. Cannon to explain his findings in animal experiments in the Harvard Physiological Laboratory. It was an extension of the concept of "milieu interne" (constant internal environment) developed by the noted French physiologist Claude Bernard, and it denoted the tendency of the organism to maintain certain physiological variables in the body within narrow limits. These are regulated by the autonomic nervous system.

Few of us realize how exact must be the conditions in our bodies to sustain life. The blood, for example, must be maintained at a slightly alkaline level, between pH 7.35 and 7.45. To accomplish this, the body is supplied with several buffer systems — the bicarbonate, phosphate, hemoglobin, and plasma protein systems — which maintain the alkalinity at this level.

The body must oxidize food stored in the liver and the muscles at all times, to supply energy for the vital processes and for movement. The heat thus produced is of great importance to us in the cooler seasons of the year. During the warm months, however, the body must lose large amounts of heat to cool the body. This is accomplished through expiring warm air through the lungs, to some extent by radiation from the surface and by warm liquid and solid

---

4. *The Eye As an Optical Instrument* (American Scientific Affiliation), p. 16.

wastes leaving the body, but principally through perspiration, as each tiny cubic centimeter of water gives off 539 calories of heat when evaporated from the skin. The heat-regulating center in the hypothalamus, at the base of the brain, keeps these processes in such delicate balance that the temperature of the body normally is kept at approximately 98.6° F winter and summer. The body can tolerate deviations of several degrees, but not for a long time. Above 105° F the body begins to form its own toxins, which create further obstacles that the body must overcome to recover. While I was an intern, a young man in critical condition with meningitis produced an axillary (under-the-arm) temperature of 107.8° F (to which an additional degree is added to conform to oral temperature). This, however, was soon forced down to below 105°. By the grace of God he recovered, and I still remember the smile on his face, so long tensed and comatose, as he walked out of the hospital after being released.

This same regulatory control is seen in the hormones, the chemical regulators of the body. These in turn depend on hormones from the pituitary gland, the master gland of the body, to stimulate their formation and release into the blood. For example, the thyrotrophic hormone in the pituitary gland stimulates the thyroid gland to produce thyroxin. When the concentration of thyroxin in the blood reaches a certain level, however, the pituitary gland is inhibited in its release of thyrotrophic hormone, so that the thyroxin concentration remains within normal limits. Too much thyroxin would make us nervous and thin; too little would make us sluggish and obese. This regulative device controls similarly the adrenal hormones, the ovarian hormones, and the growth hormone.

Water and minerals dissolved in the blood must also remain in balance. If insufficient water is taken in for more than a few days, or if too much is lost from the body (as in diarrhea), dangerous dehydration results. On the other hand, if the kidneys do not eliminate sufficient water and wastes, these accumulate in the blood, so that the tissues become water-logged and poisons increase in the blood to life-threatening levels. If potassium in the blood is too low, nausea, constipation, and "skipped beats" of the heart may result; if it is too high, the heart may stop beating. If the calcium concentration is too low, the muscles will go into spasm (tetany), causing severe cramps; if it is too high, the heart may go into "cardiac standstill." The viscosity of the blood is also limited in degree of fluctuation allowable. If it rises too high, the flow becomes sluggish and clots may form within the blood vessels; if it is too thin, hemorrhages result.

When the body dies, the protoplasm undergoes autolysis; that is, it is digested by the enzymes present which, for some reason, are no longer held in check. How these enzymes in the cells are prevented from digesting the contents before, and how they are turned loose when the "spark of life" is gone, has never been satisfactorily explained. It remains one of the unsolved mysteries of our Creator.

Vital Organs

The Liver

The liver was so named by the ancients because they believed it to be essential to life. Because of the large amounts of blood in its tissues and the number and large size of vessels entering and leaving it, it was once thought to be the organ responsible for the circulation of the blood. It is not, but when studying medical physiology, I was impressed with the many functions necessary to life that are performed in the liver.

First, *it manufactures many important substances.* It forms glycogen, the starchy storage form of carbohydrate, from glucose. It produces fibrinogen and prothrombin for the clotting mechanism of the blood. It makes albumin and globulin, which maintain the oncotic (osmotic) pressure of the blood, which is so necessary for the return of fluids and solutes to the heart from the tissues. Globulins are also necessary in antibody formation, to fight off infectious diseases. It produces bile which enables proper digestion of fats and the absorption of vitamin K. Cholesterol, the primary building block from which the hormones are synthesized, is manufactured in the liver. Glucose is produced here by "glyconeogenesis" from amino acids absorbed from the small intestine.

Second, *it is a chemical converter.* Amino acids are deaminated (the nitrogen with two hydrogen atoms is removed), so that the rest of the molecule can be used to form glucose, which man can then utilize for energy. It contributes blood sugar from carbohydrate stores. It converts ammonia to urea, which can then be removed by the kidneys safely.

Third, *it is a detoxifier.* Substances absorbed from the intestine, like phenol, indole, salicylic acid, menthol, and camphor, are rendered harmless in the liver by chemical change. This is a most important and necessary function.

Fourth, *it is the site where many substances are stored,* such as glucose (as glycogen), fat, and vitamin A.

Finally, by destroying or inactivating excess hormones which cause sodium and water to accumulate in the tissues, *it prevents edema.* How appropriate that it is called the "live-r"!

The Heart

The heart is the engine of the body, for by its action it forces food, water, and oxygen to needy tissues and "draws" away excess water and waste into the veins. It is composed of two upper atria (formerly called auricles) and two lower ventricles. The two atria beat in unison, as do the two ventricles a little later in the cycle.

Although it is seemingly tireless, the heart rests beween beats to keep its muscle fibers rested and in good repair. When a person rests for only 24 hours during an illness, the reduced rate allows the heart to save 20,000 beats to conserve energy to fight disease.

The heart is supplied with fuel and oxygen from the blood, and with amino acids for tissue repair, through the coronary arteries. It never needs oiling and normally never needs spare parts. It continues to beat approximately 72 times per minute, hour after hour, day after day, year after year, and, if given proper care, may serve us over many decades, even for a century, in which case it would beat 3,786,912,000 times.

The five quarts of blood usually present in an adult must be pumped through a network of vessels which total twelve thousand miles in length, the distance from New York City to Hong Kong via the Panama Canal. The total volume of blood pumped by the heart in one year is about 650,000 gallons.

The total length and small diameters of the smaller vessels afford considerable resistance that must be overcome by the force of the heart beat. In only twelve hours, it generates enough energy to lift, one foot from the ground, a tank car of sixty-five tons! This simple little engine, weighing little more than one-half pound, is a tribute to efficiency in design; it reflects the wisdom and power of our Lord, by whom "we are fearfully and wonderfully made" (Ps. 139:14).

Part II

General Refutation
of Evolution

4

The Theory of Evolution

How pleasing it would be to the flesh to allow our case to rest on the positive evidences for a divine Creator. Yet we know that the message of the gospel is both positive and negative, and that those who witness to it are both to exhort to sound doctrine and to refute false doctrine. "All Scripture is given by inspiration of God, and is profitable for doctrine, for reproof, for correction, for instruction in righteousness" (II Tim. 3:16). It is not only for doctrine and instruction, but also for reproof and correction. We shall examine the theory of evolution first from the scientific standpoint and then from the scriptural.

The need to examine the doctrine of evolution is obvious. It is being presented in popular magazines, scientific journals, and newspapers. It is being force-fed to millions of children in the public schools, beginning in the lower grades. Many states now require the subject to be taught in their curricula. It is even propagated, during discussion in many nominally Christian churches and church schools. It is an issue that we cannot escape, one which we should face without hesitation and without fear, but with the facts at hand.

The concept of evolution is first, last, and always a theory. Once again, we emphasize the importance of distinguishing between theory and fact. Although an evolutionist is one who "believes in" the theory (that is, believes it is factual), yet he may disagree widely and at times heatedly with his fellow evolutionists about specific details. Therefore, any description or definition of evolution should be given with this understanding.

Evolution may be defined as the theory that plants and animals have undergone gradual changes in structure and function from simple species to complex creatures, the greatest complexity being found in man.

In theory, evolution began eons ago when there were no living plants and animals, only inorganic sterile rocks, soils, and mixtures and solutions of all these. At a certain time and in a certain place, the inorganic mixtures and solutions, with their accompanying gases, were in just the right proportions so that, under the energy stimulus of light, heat, or lightning, the dead elements combined in such a way that the first living protoplasm was instantaneously formed. From this primordial ooze came the first living creature which survived and multiplied. After many generations, it manifested structural changes significant enough to constitute a new species. This in turn developed into a still more complex creature. In this way one could explain — on a purely mechanistic basis, if he so chose — the sudden appearance of large, virus-like molecules, which on augmentation of their structure with cytoplasm, graded into one-celled animals and plants such as *Amoeba, Euglena,* and *Chlamydomonas* (fig. 5). From these, simple Metazoa of several to many cells developed; these in turn gave rise to the sponges, followed in order by the coelenterates (as the jellyfish), the flatworms, the roundworms, the segmented worms, the arthropods (as the insects), the mollusks, the echinoderms (as the starfish), the chor-

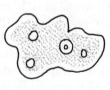
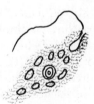
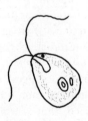

AMOEBA   EUGLENA   CHLAMYDOMONAS

Fig. 5. One-celled organisms

dates, and finally the vertebrates. Among the vertebrates the fishes supposedly developed into the amphibia, the reptiles, the birds, and the mammals, respectively, with man being the crowning but still unfinished product of the evolutionary tree. From the simplest plants, such as *Chlamydomonas,* developed the thallophytes (such as the more complex algae, the fungi, and the lichens), which were followed by the bryophytes (mosses and liverworts), pteridophytes (such as the ferns), and finally the spermatophytes (the seed-bearing plants, the most complex of which bear flowers).

Even the first step in the hypothesis, involving the formation of the first living protoplasm, lacks substantiation and raises a number of questions.

The first is, "What is the source of nitrogen, a necessary building block in living protoplasm, in this synthesis?" This has necessitated another modern theory which postulates that the atmosphere at that time contained large concentrations of ammonia, hydrogen, and methane. However, in any significant concentration, ammonia is so toxic that such newly formed organisms would soon perish. The evolutionist then finds it necessary to further speculate that the ammonia must have been converted into elemental nitrogen almost instantaneously! Inasmuch as light, temperature, moisture, and other meteorologic conditions would vary greatly from place to place on the earth, the idea that all of the ammonia in the atmosphere would be depleted suddenly should be acceptable only to the credulous. Further, this theory requires a complete absence of oxygen in the air, meaning that the oxygen which is so plentiful today must have come from oxides which were subsequently reduced to pure metals. However, most of our metals in the earth's crust are present as oxides rather than in a reduced form, and water, present in such tremendous quantities in our oceans and atmosphere, is actually an oxide of hydrogen. The theory is not consistent with these facts.

The English chemist, Sir William Tilden, wrote in a letter to the *London Times:* "I venture to think that no chemist will be prepared to suggest a process by which . . . if by a complex series of changes a compound of this kind [i.e., proteid] were conceivably produced, that it would present the characters of living protoplasm. Far be it from any man of science to affirm that any given set of phenomena is not a fit subject of inquiry. . . . In the present instance, however, it appears to me that this is not a field . . . in which chemistry is likely to afford any assistance whatever." The author who quotes him continues forcibly: "In any case, the idea that a chaos of unassorted elements and undirected forces could succeed where the skill of the chemist fails is preposterous. No known or conceivable process or group of processes, at work in inorganic nature, is equal to the task. Chance is an explanation only for minds insensible to the beauty of organic life."[1]

Botany professor Frank B. Salisbury of Utah State University has determined that the formation of a single molecule of DNA (deoxyribonucleic acid) is mathematically unlikely. Taking into account such factors as protein molecular size, ocean depth, DNA concentration, and rate of reproduction and mutation, he states, "Only one molecule of over 10^{500} would be acceptable . . . and after four billion years . . . the chances are still immeasurably small (10^{415}) that a proper DNA molecule would be produced in this time."[2]

He refers to Quastler's similar calculations, which also indicate "essentially no probability,"[3] and the fact that, although in a DNA chain, only a few sites would be active: (1) even if only two amino acids produce an active site, every protein would be covered by many if not most of them; (2) the "inactive" amino acids in the chain are important because they help make up the *sequence* of the chain, as proven by denaturation experiments. He continues, "Special creation or directed evolution would solve the complexity of the gene,"[4] adding that this, of course, would be beyond the realm of experiment.

Further, it is apparent that the formation of DNA is not equivalent to the origination of life. So we have many voices joining in testifying to one great truth: natural processes argue for a divine Designer and Creator, rather than for life beginning by mere chance.

Another, equally formidable question is, "What was the first 'creature'?"

If it were a virus, it would undoubtedly remain a virus and develop into nothing else, decomposing when environmental conditions became prohibitive. Why is this true? It has long been known that viruses cannot multiply except when residing within

1. Quoted by George B. O'Toole, *The Case Against Evolution* (New York: Macmillan, 1925), pp. 151f.

2. "Natural Selection and the Complexity of the Gene," *Nature*, 224 (Oct. 25, 1969), pp. 342f.

3. *The Emergence of Biological Organization* (New Haven: Yale Univ. Press, 1964).

4. "Natural Selection," p. 343.

living cells of plants and animals (which would be conspicuous by their absence). Inasmuch as viruses cannot synthesize living protoplasm, many ardent evolutionists themselves have conceded that the viruses are not living entities at all, but are of the order of complex enzymes capable of catalyzing their own synthesis but lacking cytoplasm.

If the first creature were an animal, it would most certainly perish from lack of food, for the ultimate foods of animals are plants.

If it were a simple plant, such as the genus *Chlamydomonas,* it would at first seem to have a much better chance (though not in an ammoniated atmosphere). However, the food supply would still be prohibitive without any organic matter present, unless the concentration of all necessary elements were present as dissolved salts in the right concentration to prevent the cell membrane from shrinking or stretching too much, and *continued* to be present in these delicate proportions for enough centuries, or even millions of years, for this plant to evolve into the next higher organism. This would assume also that climatic conditions remain sufficiently encouraging for the organism to continue living for this period of time.

If a green plant like one of the *Chlamydomonas* were the first creature, it would require the instantaneous and simultaneous creation of a cell membrane, a nucleus, cytoplasmic contents, and that most complex substance we know as chlorophyll. For us to believe that this could happen without any Designer formulating and fashioning its structure would seem to require considerable gullibility, in contrast with the belief that the plants and animals around us are the handiwork of God's creative power.

The belief that God created one protoplasmic mass and then threw the key away, allowing the laws of chance to take over and govern His domain by evolutionary methods, has, as we shall see, neither scientific nor scriptural evidence to support it.

5

Comparative Anatomy

As now taught in the typical college, comparative anatomy promotes the theory of organic evolution. Even for medical students, the laboratory course has little value except for some experience in dissection. It seemed odd to me that we were asked to examine the slides of very simple marine animals such as the tunicates and amphioxus, and were expected to agree that they were pivotal in the evolution of the vertebrates because they have a cartilaginous cord superficially resembling the notochord in the embryo of mammals. We carefully dissected preserved cats to find and identify the bones, muscles, blood vessels, nerves, and external organs which resemble, in some ways, those of man.

In the classroom we were instructed day after day on the similarities in structure between man and the lower animals. For example, the giraffe and the mouse both have seven vertebrae in the neck, despite the great difference in their respective sizes, the giraffe neck being nearly eight feet long. The number of neck vertebrae in man is also seven. In the same way, the arms of man correspond to the front legs of the cow and the frog, to the wings of the bird, and to the pectoral fins of the fish. The horse and the dog both have well-developed muscles to move the ears; man has a similar set of muscles, though they are much weaker in function. That these similarities exist between man and the beasts can be illustrated with many examples, and in the setting of a classroom which is evolution-oriented and in which crass propaganda is steadily repeated, countless thousands of students each year are led to believe in evolution. They are taught repeatedly that similarity in structure proves a common ancestry. Instructors assume from the beginning that evolution has been proven.

We were made to feel that it is certain that complex animals come from simpler animals by gradual, evolutionary change, as diagrammed in figure 6.

We were given many examples of structures in lower animals that resemble man. The proboscis monkey, for example, has a nose somewhat resembling an oversized human nose and the lemur has hands resembling man's. Yet, when carefully analyzed, the examples weakened, not strengthened, their argument, for if man actually ascended an evolutionary scale through these inferior beasts, there should be one species that is most like man in all these respects. The inability to find such a species in which these structures show a *fusion* of organ characteristics pointing in the direction of man indicates that these are merely chance similarities. The lemur, embarrassing as it may be to the evolutionists, is not even classified as an ape. The "feet" of all the lesser and greater apes are merely a second pair of hands, and are not designed for walking. The feet of bears and raccoons are better designed for standing than the apes' (the dancing bears of Europe illustrate this facility well) ; the gorilla can stand only with difficulty, stretching his thumb-like great toe sideways to the limit to gain stability in the erect position.

Despite the comparative anatomist's outward appearance of self-confidence, nothing demonstrates his uncertainty more than the fact that he is constantly changing his classifications, which are

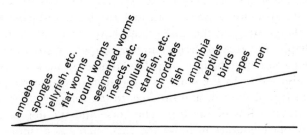

Fig. 6. The "evolutionary scale"

based on comparative anatomy. When I studied zoology, the Echinodermata (spiny-skinned animals such as starfish and sea urchins) were considered quite primitive, and were placed between the round worms and the segmented worms on the evolutionary scale. Now it is admitted that this group does not demonstrate a close similarity to any of the other phyla of invertebrates, and on the basis of their development are placed next to the chordates! (See fig. 8.) The great gap between the vertebrates and the invertebrates (with their external skeletons and ventral nerve cords) is so great that no satisfactory explanation has been given to justify the supposedly smooth gradation up the evolutionary scale.

The evolutionist experiences difficulties when he presses his theory that similar external structures prove a genuinely close relationship. For example, the shark, the mackerel, and the porpoise exhibit very similar, streamlined, torpedo-shaped bodies with a single posterior fin or flipper. Yet they are representative of three different groups: the cartilaginous fishes, the bony fishes, and the far more complex mammals, respectively.

Similarly, flowering plants like the water shield, mermaid weed, water crowfoot, lake cress, coon tail, and water milfoil have one thing in common; they are totally or partly submerged in water, the submerged leaves being finely dissected or "fern-like." So similar are these submerged leaves that our class in aquatic plants prepared an identification key to help distinguish them readily. Yet, only two belong to the same family, and their dissected leaf forms superficially resemble chara and nitella, both of which are often classified with the algae, the simplest, most "primitive" of the plant phyla.

Some evolutionists call this "convergence." Others term it "evolutionary parallelism." Dr. Charles Girton, while teaching plant physiology at Purdue University, once remarked with a chuckle (when a student's classroom demonstration was not going well), that in research it is not so important for one to succeed in an experiment as to give an explanation for its failure. The evolutionist learned this long ago; furthermore, when he cannot explain it, he gives it a name worthy of a scientist!

How then do we explain the similarities that do exist? Actually, these similarities *argue just as strongly for a common Creator* as for a common ancestry, making them in perfect harmony with the biblical account.

For example, all the schools in the city of my boyhood were designed by the same architect, a local man who was highly regarded. He also designed some of the newer churches in the city; these were distinctive and easily recognized since they all looked like schools! In the same way, we may expect some similarities in structure between man and animals, because they have been designed and molded by the same Architect. "All things were made by him; and without him was not any thing made that was made . . ." (John 1:3).

6

Comparative Embryology

Embryology is the study of the development of an organism from the time the egg is fertilized at conception until birth (although, when applied to humans, the term *embryo* is reserved for the earlier stages and *fetus* is used for the more advanced stages). These earlier stages are diagrammed in figure 7.

These stages are the same in all vertebrates at the beginning of development. The evolutionist argues that one-celled animals (Protozoa) and plants did not develop beyond the first stage. It could be argued that the desmids (two-celled plants) stopped with the two-celled stage, that bacteria like Sarcina stop with the eight-celled stage; that Volvox, a simple water plant, resembles the blastula and thus did not develop beyond that stage; and that the jellyfish turned off at the gastrula stage.

Further, the lancelet (amphioxus), which has a cartilaginous rod similar to the notochord of the embryo, stopped developing at that stage. With the development of a simple two-chambered heart and gills, the fish turned off from the developmental tree. With a three-chambered heart and simple lungs, the amphibia (e.g., the frogs) terminate their development. With the partial formation of a dividing septum in the single ventricle, the reptiles leave the common route of development. With the four-chambered heart and

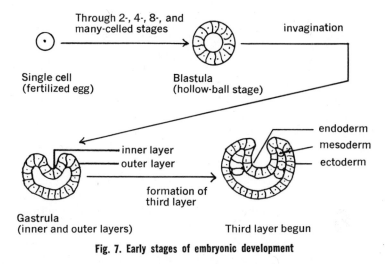

Fig. 7. Early stages of embryonic development

feathers, the birds cease their development and with hair and milk formation, the mammals stop at the very apex of development.

Some similarities can often be observed, but they require careful evaluation. For example, the two-celled desmids are infinitely more complex than the eight-celled colonies of Sarcina, and many Protozoa are more complex than either of them (fig. 8). Further, even as similarity in adult forms argues for a common Creator, so the similarity in *development* of the adult form argues just as eloquently for the Master Planner Himself, who has said in no uncertain terms: "For all those things hath mine hand made, and all those things have been, saith the Lord . . ." (Isa. 66:2).

However, the evolutionist attempts to use the study of embryology to prove that each embryo, in its development from the one-celled stage to the adult, passes through stages that parallel each successive step in the evolutionary development of that particular species. He "sees," therefore, in the embryo of man, the "protozoan stage," the

PARAMECIUM   COSMARUM   SARCINA

Fig. 8. One-, two-, and eight-celled organisms

"segmented worm stage," the "fish stage," the "tail stage," and the "hair stage" — and points to these as proof that man has, over many centuries, gone through these same stages in gradually developing from a one-celled organism to an adult species. Let us consider the "proof" that he offers for this theory.

The "protozoan stage." This stage is said to be found in the male reproductive cell (sperm) since it is motile (capable of moving) and actually swims to the egg. However, if it were parallel to Protozoa, it would be so in both function and structure. As a matter of fact, the sperm has no structural parallel in all of protozoology; it is well over ninety percent nucleus, whereas the protozoan nucleus is relatively small and can be seen only with difficulty in many species, even when stained. Nor has it any comparable representative physiologically, for it has only one function and that is to fertilize the egg and contribute its nuclear (and to some extent, cytoplasmic) material to it. It has no independent life, cannot assimilate food particles, and cannot reproduce itself.

The "segmented worm stage." The similarity between somites, the symmetrical blocks of tissue which can be seen along the back (dorsal) aspect of the human embryo, and the segments in the adult earthworm are cited as proof that somewhere in man's ancestry he passed through a worm stage.

In his widely-used embryology text, Leslie Arey says, "This segmental arrangement brings to mind the serial divisions or metameres of an earthworm's body. In the worm each metamere similarly contains a ganglion of the nerve cord, a muscle segment, and pairs of nerves, blood vessels, and excretory tubules."[1] However, comparison of carefully drawn cross-sections of an earthworm and a human embryo (see fig. 9) show impressive differences, so much so that some students, when confronted with this comparison in our medical embryology class, were visibly shaken in their view, which they had absorbed from teachers of evolution.

Arey acknowledges "differences between the metamerism of a worm and of the vertebrate embryo; in the worm it is complete and both external and internal; in the vertebrate it is incomplete ventrally, and purely internal."[2]

Other and perhaps more basic differences also exist. The similarities pointed out are the somites, the nephrotomes (kidney buds),

---

1. *Developmental Anatomy* (Philadelphia: W. B. Saunders, 1965), p. 93.
2. Ibid.

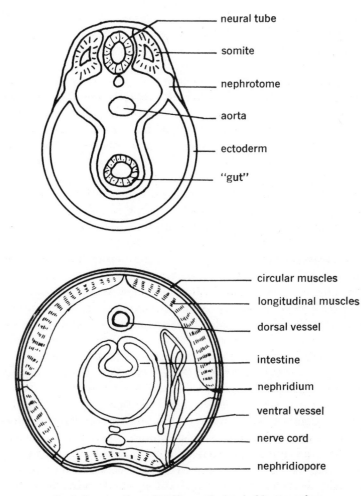

neural tube

somite

nephrotome

aorta

ectoderm

"gut"

circular muscles

longitudinal muscles

dorsal vessel

intestine

nephridium

ventral vessel

nerve cord

nephridiopore

Fig. 9. Cross sections of earthworm (top) and of human embryo

pairs of nerves, and the blood vessels. However, even these, when scrutinized, are more dissimilar than similar to the earthworm's structure. The general orientation of the somites is horizontal, and these are found only in the upper (dorsal) region of the embryo. In contrast, the worm's metameres are comprised of strong muscular masses, the bulk of which run longitudinally, and of circular muscles that are much thinner. Further, both of these completely surround the internal organs, being found ventrally (below) and laterally, as well as dorsally. The nephridia (simple kidney-like organs) of the earthworm are distinctly ventral, while the corresponding nephrotome of the embryo is decidedly dorsal. The aorta is central in the embryo, while both a dorsal vessel and smaller ventral vessel are found in the earthworm.

Most important is the fact that, whereas the worm's nerve cord is ventral, as in all invertebrates, the corresponding neural tube in the embryo is dorsal from the very beginning of its appearance until development is complete. Hence, any attempt to identify the embryo with any invertebrate, let alone the earthworm, is hardly scientific.

As Dr. Ferenc Kiss has concluded, ". . . it is necessary for the evolutionists — in order to maintain their theory — to collect only similarities and to neglect the numerous differences."[3]

Cleveland Hickman, in comparing the arthropods and vertebrates with the earthworms, concedes, "The fact that these groups have metamerism (segments) does not necessarily indicate a close relationship between them, for the condition may have arisen independently by convergent evolution."[4] However, this fact argues just as strongly for an independent special creation. His statement is just another way of saying that metameres or somites do not necessarily indicate common ancestry. Therefore, they should not be submitted as evidence for an evolutionary process at all.

The "fish stage." If I were to discuss only one "stage," it would be this one, for it is this stage that, by all odds, receives the greatest emphasis in comparative embryology. All vertebrate embryos look much the same in their earlier stages, much as all buildings look much the same when the basement is poured and the foundation is laid. Later, however, significant differences appear. Six weeks after fertilization, the embryo has a relatively large head with only stumps where the arms and legs will appear. In what appears to be the neck region are the pharyngeal pouches which, to some scientists, resemble the gills of a fish. (See fig. 10.) In their enthusiasm to promote the idea that man has evolved from lower animals, many evolutionists refer to these as "gill slits." Newman, for example, writes: "At one stage they are all alike in their hearts, arteries, gill-slits, and various other structures . . ."[5] A little observa-

---

3. *Facts and Fallacies of Evolution* (Chicago: Inter-Varsity Christian Fellowship), p. 7.
4. *Integrated Principles of Zoology* (St. Louis: C. V. Mosby, 1955), p. 246.
5. Horatio-Hackett Newman, *Evolution Yesterday and Today* (Williams & Wilkins Co., 1932). Quoted in *Composition and Research, Problems in the Evolu-*

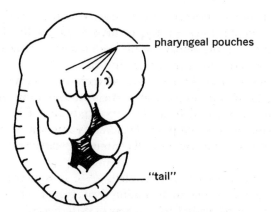

Fig. 10. Vertebrate embryo of six weeks' gestation

tion, however, shows this term, "gill-slits," to be grossly inaccurate: they are not gills, and they are not even slits!

To deserve the term *gills,* they would have to parallel those organs at least in structure and function. In structure, true fish gills are used for external respiration. Inasmuch as oxygen is only slightly soluble in water (about three percent), gills must take up this small amount very rapidly to supply enough oxygen for the oxidation of food, which in turn makes possible the strong, rapid movements essential to swimming. The gill possesses thousands of capillaries which provide an immense surface through which oxygen can be absorbed in large quantities. Any experienced fisherman realizes that the gills underneath the external flap (operculum) are blood red from these capillaries. However, the pharyngeal clefts of the embryo do not exhibit any such proliferation of capillaries. In function, the pharyngeal pouches at no time have any relationship to the respiratory system. Throughout the period of embryonic development and up to the time of delivery of the newborn baby, the latter is entirely dependent on the two umbilical arteries for its oxygen supply. These arteries, with the umbilical vein, make up the internal vessels coursing through the umbilical cord, which is the lifeline connecting the embryo with the lining of the mother's uterus. Oxygen from the mother's blood, which passes through the villous connections of the placenta and into the umbilical arteries, sustains life up to the time of birth. Then

tionary Theory by A. Wayne Colver and Robert J. Stevick (New York: The Bobbs-Merrill Co., 1963), p. 110.

the newborn baby, after its first early cries, gasps for air, shifting from mother's oxygen to oxygen in the air. This critical and dramatic moment proceeds ordinarily with perfect timing.

Further, as we have said, the pharyngeal clefts are not "slits" at all. They are always covered with a membrane comprised of at least three layers (endoderm, mesoderm, and ectoderm), and no liquid ever passes through them.

Finally, if this were to prove that man came from the fish, the fish should not have these same pharyngeal clefts *before* development of the gills, but it does. Thus the attempt to identify these clefts with gills breaks down completely.

The "tail stage." Some evolutionists argue that, at six weeks gestation, the embryo has a tail, which in fact exceeds the legs in length. At this stage the embryo is, by comparison with the newborn, greatly distorted and bizarre in shape, with a large head and a heart relatively larger than in maturity. The embryo is the size of only a pea, and the pointed extension of the embryo called a tail is really not one at all in structure. A true tail, as found in the ape and more simple mammals, is supported by additional caudal vertebrae. The embryo has none of these; man never has more than thirty-three (five make up the sacrum and four the coccyx). This part of the body is a temporary extension containing the normal vertebrae and part of the intestine or colon, the anal aperture being near the end of the "tail."

The "hair stage." It is said that at one stage man is thickly covered with hair, indicating his ape-like ancestry. The hair referred to is lanugo, silky hairs which are much finer than those of the adult. They begin to disappear at the eighth month of gestation. They are so fine they can scarcely be seen and, after the eighth month of gestation, are lost from most of the body. They are retained after birth only on the face, where they can be seen upon close inspection around the eyes and on the ears. They are always nonpigmented, even in the brunette. At no time do they give to the embryo an ape-like appearance. They are quite different from the larger, stronger hairs that replace them, and even more so from those of the ape, which they are alleged to resemble.

Having considered the fallacies of the arguments from embryology which are alleged to support evolution, we turn now to some positive arguments in opposition to the theory itself.

Dr. Kiss, a Hungarian physician engaged in medical research in several fields, recalls the outstanding paper, "The Problem of

Man's Development," read by Dr. L. Bolk, late professor of anatomy in Amsterdam. Dr. Bolk, an evolutionist, read this paper at the German Anatomical Congress in Freiburg in 1926. The more than twenty years of investigation upon which it was based provided evidence that man, rather than being at the top of an evolutionary scale, is in many respects *physically inferior* to the lower animals.

Man requires twenty to twenty-four years to reach maturity, whereas the ape requires but three or four. This slow development, with a long period of dependence, is called retardation by Dr. Bolk. The fetal hair (lanugo) referred to previously is replaced by a strong, mature type of hair on the head and a few small areas; the remainder of the body is covered sparsely, and often hardly at all. This condition of man would seem to reflect *fetalization*.

The mature spine of man tends to follow the ventral curve of the embryo, whereas in the ape the spinal curve is stretched so as to open dorsally (above), which is structurally more efficient and mature. (See fig. 11.)

In the same way, the human body keeps essentially the embryonal postition of the parts of the head, whereas in lower animals the head is stretched out (see fig. 12), an apparently superior structural relationship.

Other examples of human inferiorities, in the physical sense,

Fig. 11. Spinal curves of human (left) and subhuman embryos

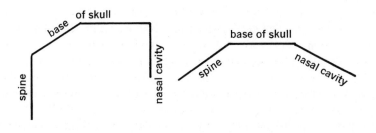

Fig. 12. Embryonal structures of head in man (left) and beast

may be cited. A surgical site that requires eight to ten days for complete healing in man takes but three or four days in lower animals. The greater resistance of animals to disease and their more rapid recovery from it are well known.

The congenital abnormalities of man are all due to local retardation of development. "We do not find any sign in human embryology which would suggest progress from the present condition," writes Kiss. In the same manner, mutations in the germ plasm ordinarily produce only degenerative forms and not progressive changes in the fetus.

Kiss summarized Bolk's observations as proof that: (1) the human body is not on the top of the scale of organic evolution; (2) the biology of man is distinct from all animals, including the apes; (3) the ape belongs, in all his biological and embryological characteristics, with the lower animals.

The physical inferiority of man, however, is not as sweeping as even these men would have us believe. I have frequently heard the claim that many of man's structural ills, such as arthritis, scoliosis, kyphosis, lordosis, and dislocation of joints (e.g., the cervical vertebral joints and the sacroiliac joints), are "due to man's accommodation to the erect position." The inference is that the four-footed beasts possess a physiologically superior posture. Actually, the lower animals are subject to the same ills. Stiff and arthritic joints, for example, are found in many of them at a much earlier age than is usual for man. Man's longevity, almost unsurpassed in the animal kingdom, testifies to his structural and anatomical soundness. The point is that we find no *consistent* pattern of a gradually increasing complexity that ends in man.

The superiority of man is not so much in his physical strength and effficiency (as should be the case if he had evolved from lower animals) as in his far superior central nervous system, which vastly increases his capacity to learn and to communicate. The average weight of man's brain, for example, is three times that of the ape, and it gives him mental powers markedly superior to those of all lower animals. Not only can he alter and improve his physical environment, he can also communicate with Him who created man's brain and sustains it to His glory.

This is the mind which is made new (renewed) by the Spirit of Christ at conversion (Eph. 4:23) and which expresses the transformed life of the believer as the Spirit calls forth His fruit in daily life, in both word and deed.

7

Vestigial Organs

A vestige is a trace or remnant of something which formerly exerted an influential role. Organs like the tonsils, appendix, and the thymus gland are claimed by the evolutionists to be "vestigial" — that is, degenerate remnants of organs which were useful to allegedly more primitive ancestors but which have become useless.

But the more we learn, with the help of medical research, about the body's many organs the less any organ appears vestigial, or superfluous to the body's normal activities. At one time even the thyroid gland was thought to be vestigial; now we know it determines the personality of the patient, whether he will be energetic or lethargic, lean or obese, nervous or calm.

Let us take a closer look at the organs that are claimed to be vestigial.

The Tonsils

The tonsils, part of the lymphatic system, are the guardians of the throat, which is the port of entry of most infectious diseases. In the lymphatic tissue of the tonsils, bacteria are strained from the lymph, and huge concentrations of white blood cells (lymphocytes) ingest them, much as amoebas ingest food particles. As long as the body is in reasonably good health, the tonsils function well and are an asset to our health. They should not be removed, therefore, unless repeated infections threaten the patient with rheumatic fever or middle ear infection, or unless chronic infection becomes a source of toxins in the body and a cesspool encouraging acute flare-ups from viral and bacterial assault. Dr. Robert A. Good of the University of Minnesota Medical School Hospitals emphasized to the American Academy of Pediatrics in Chicago that during infancy the tonsils also help to establish the body's ability to produce disease-fighting antibodies. He advised that, until more is known about them, they should not be removed indiscriminately at any age. "We should be extremely conservative in dealing with these systems which we do not understand." He was supported in his stand against routine tonsillectomies by Dr. Vincent Larkin, chief of pediatrics at Brooklyn's Methodist Hospital.

Three New York physicians, Drs. Vianna, Greenwald, and Davies, studying patients with Hodgkins disease from twenty-five hospitals in Long Island, New York, concluded that tonsillectomy appeared to increase susceptibility to the disease by approximately three times.[1]

Further, an associate professor in pediatric allergy at New York Medical College reminded the New Jersey Medical Society at their annual meeting that, "We have all been told that 'My child's asthma developed after the T & A was done.' . . . the association of surgery and asthma is too frequent to be called coincidence."[2]

The Appendix

The appendix can be removed and we can continue living an essentially normal life. This has misled many to conclude that it is vestigial, but such a conclusion is most superficial. One may lose a finger or even a hand and not only live but prosper in his work, living to the age of 100 years, but the finger and hand are not therefore vestigial. As long as they were in the body they were put to efficient use.

A study of the appendix reveals several important structures histologically: (1) Within the wall of the appendix are large areas of lymphatic tissue, or nodules. Maximow and Bloom, in their widely used textbook in histology, agree that this "lymphatic tissue

---

1. N. J. Vianna, Peter Greenwald, and U.N. Davies, *P. Lancet* 1: 7696. Quoted in *Medical World News* (April 2, 1971), p. 48c.
2. Dr. Maclyn Cagan, *Infectious Diseases* (Sept. 30, 1972), p. 10.

is similar to that of the tonsils."[3] (2) The appendix, situated near the junction of the small intestine with the colon, appears to guard somewhat the intestines in the region of the cecum where the colon begins. Emptying into the lumen of the appendix are large numbers of glands (crypts) of Liberkuhn. These contain goblet cells which produce mucus, a lubricant found also in the lining of the small intestine and colon. The writer is acquainted with patients who have suffered constipation after an appendectomy, possibly for this reason. (3) The appendix is rich in argentaffin (staining easily with silver salts) cells. Their nature and function have long been obscure, but "recent evidence indicates that they are . . . endocrine, and are now known to be rich in hydroxytryptophan."[4]

Perhaps an even more important function has been coming to light only recently. Dr. Howard R. Bierman, clinical professor of medicine, Loma Linda University School of Medicine, Santa Barbara, California, has studied several hundred patients with leukemia, Hodgkin's disease, cancer of the colon, and cancer of the ovaries. He found that 84 percent of these had had the appendix removed years earlier. In a control group without cancer, only 25 percent had had it removed. He concludes that the organ may be "an immunologic organ whose premature removal during its functional period permits leukemia and other related forms of cancer to begin their development." He credits this to the lymphoid tissue which "may secrete antibodies which protect the body against attacking viral agents."[5]

The Thymus

Scientists have done an about-face in their attitude toward this gland, which is located beneath the upper portion of the breast bone (sternum). The idea that it is useless has been completely exploded by very competent scientists. It is now recognized as the master gland of the intricate immunity sysem of the body.

Dr. Robert A. Good and Richard L. Varco at the University of Minnesota discovered that a patient whose thymus was destroyed by a benign tumor suffered from acquired lack of gamma globulin in his blood. Because this substance is essential in antibody formation, he had no resistance, suffering seventeen bouts of pneumonia

---

3. Alexander Maximow and Wm. Bloom, *Textbook of Histology* (Philadelphia: W. B. Saunders Co., 1957).
4. *MD Magazine* (March, 1970), p. 240.
5. *Science Digest* (June, 1966) pp. 31f.

in two years. Upon removing the thymus from newborn rabbits, scientists have found the animals unable to manufacture antibodies and normal lymphocytes. Similar research in England, Australia, and Sweden has supported these findings.

Dr. Robert Kretchner and others at Harvard University Medical Schools, studying infants whose thymus glands failed to develop properly and who suffered frequent overwhelming infections, have come to the same conclusion.[6]

Dr. Raphael Levey, in a review on thymus function, explains that the thymus is the seedbed of the lymphocytes, sending them out as "colonists" to the spleen and lymph nodes to mature and multiply there. It is aided by a thymic hormone; in fact, three separate hormones have been isolated from the gland's secretion. He also advances some evidence that the secretional elements may destroy cancer cells (as foreign bodies) in an early stage.[7]

With the increase in knowledge about these allegedly useless organs, the argument from "vestigial" organs fades as the morning mist before the rays of the sun. Just because we do not as yet understand fully the use of these various organs, we should not question the wisdom of the Creator who put them there.

-----

6. "Congenital Aplasia of the Thymus Gland," *The New England Journal of Medicine,* 279 (Dec. 12, 1968), p. 1300.

7. "The Thymus Hormones," *Scientific American* (July, 1964), p. 213.

8

Geology

Some Basic Principles

The three main types of rocks are classified as igneous, sedimentary, and metamorphic.

Igneous rocks are formed from molten lava. Examples are: (1) pumice, which is very light and porous from formerly entrapped gases; (2) obsidian, which is heavy and glossy and virtually without pores; (3) basalt, which is moderately heavy and opaque; (4) granite, heavy rock which is a mixture of three minerals (quartz, feldspar, and mica).

Sedimentary rocks are formed by the transfer of unsettled particles from their point of origin to a distant site. Here they are laid down in layers, usually in flood waters. Examples are limestone, sandstone, shale, and conglomerate rock. Clay is sedimentary but softer than rock. Less common are rocks and soils from wind-blown loess (a silty material). Still more rare are those that are built up from layers of volcanic dust.

Metamorphic rocks are those which have come from either igneous or sedimentary origin, but which, under additional forces (presumably heat and pressure), have been fashioned into somewhat altered and heavier forms. *Metamorphic* means changed in structure. Thus gneiss is thought to be metamorphosed igneous rock; among those of sedimentary origin, marble is thought to come from limestone, slate from shale, and anthracite from bituminous coal.

Determining the Age of Rocks

For years men have speculated regarding the earth's age. As we noticed in the chapter on comparative anatomy, many teachers advocate organic evolution, but they use arguments based largely on speculations that an objective scientist would never use. In my own studies in college, I felt that the best evidence would come from sources like geology and the fossil record. A volume on the subject (loaned to me by a professor at Purdue University) began with a statement something like this: "Regardless of what we evolutionists would like to contend, there is no accurate method of determining the age of a rock." The author pointed out the unreliability of each method then used in dating rocks: sedimentation rate, fluoride absorption, cave formation, ocean levels, and salt content. The results varied from about 200 million to 900 million years. More recent than that volume, however, was the method based on the rate of emission of radioactive particles from uranium. This method, said the scientists, outdated all others and was absolutely foolproof. Now they *knew* that the age of the earth was two billion years.

However, a new method of dating has been brought forth about every decade since that time, and each time a still more ancient age is applied to this poor old terrestrial globe. Now the scientists say they only thought they knew back then, but now are *certain* that it is 4.5 billion years old! The fact that two succeeding generations of knowing scientists differ by 125 percent is not at all disconcerting to them, but it raises questions in the minds of some.

Obviously one must be able to determine the age of specific rocks in the earth's crust in order to determine the earth's age. Let us examine the methods that are used to date a rock.

When one enters the biology laboratories in a college campus, one is expected to be, and usually is, overawed by the chart on the wall that depicts geological periods of time, as presumably found in the earth's crust. Each of these periods is characterized by certain fossils found in that particular layer. (See fig. 13.)

Inasmuch as the chart has been prepared for science laboratories by trained scientists, one might conclude that it is inerrant and

ERAS	PERIODS	CHARACTERISTIC LIFE	ESTIMATED YEARS AGO
Cenozoic	Quaternary Recent epoch Pleistocene	rise of modern plants, animals, and man	25,000 975,000
	Tertiary Pliocene Miocene Oligocene Eocene Paleocene	rise of mammals and highest plant types	12,000,000 25,000,000 35,000,000 60,000,000 70,000,000
Mesozoic	Cretaceous	modernized angiosperms and insects	
	Jurassic	first (reptilian) birds, first angiosperms, highest insect forms	70,000,000 to 200,000,000
	Triassic	earliest dinosaurs, primitive mammals	
Paleozoic	Permian	first modern corals, primitive reptiles, earliest cycads	
carbon-iferous	Pennsylvanian	earliest insects, abundant spore plants	200,000,000
	Mississippian	rise of amphibians	
	Devonian	first seed plants, many boneless fishes	to
	Silurian	first land animals, rise of fishes	
	Ordovician	earliest vertebrates, primitive land plants	500,000,000
	Cambrian	all subkingdoms of invertebrates present, trilobites common	
Proterozoic	Keeweenawan	primitive water-dwelling plants and animals	500,000,000 to 1,000,000,000
	Huronian		
Archezoic	Timiskaming	oldest known life (indirect evidence)	1,000,000,000 to 1,800,000,000
	Keewatin		

Fig. 13. Geological time chart

69

beyond question. This is anything but true. The fossils mentioned are not found in orderly sequence one above another, as one might conclude, but are frequently gathered from widely separated sites. Their position on the chart is determined by their place in the supposed scheme of evolution. In short, one supposedly finds the age of a fossil by the age of the rock it is in, but the age of the rock is determined by the fossil in it! Schuchert and Pirsson said as much: "After one hundred years of endeavor, a great deal of knowledge has been worked out as to the evolutionary sequence of organisms, and this knowledge can be relied upon to *fix in turn the stratigraphical sequence* [relative order of the earth layers]."[1] Grabau, in the same text, claims: "that the modern animal and plant world has developed from *pre-existing forms . . .* has been *clearly demonstrated by the labours of the biologists.*"[2] This writer seems quite unaware that biology is a most inexact science and that it makes a flimsy platform for the geologist who attempts to pontificate concerning relative ages of strata in the earth.

The fallacy of this approach is acknowledged even by some historical geologists. One is R. H. Rastall, lecturer in economic geology at Cambridge, who agrees that geologists are arguing in a circle; the geological succession (and thus relative age) of organisms is determined by the "study of their remains embedded in the rocks, and the relative ages of the rocks are determined by the remains of organisms that they contain."[3]

This circular reasoning is most damaging to the whole evolutionary scheme, yet it is seldom even noticed by the heavily indoctrinated students in biology and geology.

Uniformitarianism Versus Catastrophism

The interpretation of the layers of the rocks in the earth has divided geologists into two groups. The older geologists regarded the sedimentary deposits to be largely laid down at the time of the great flood in the days of Noah. They concluded that they were catastrophic in origin, in that the flood was a sudden and worldwide disaster. Most evangelical Christians hold this view today.

---

1. *Textbook of Geology*, ii, p. 24. Quoted in *After Its Kind*, rev. ed., by Byron Nelson (Minneapolis: Bethany Fellowship, 1967), p. 72.
2. Ibid., p. 53.
3. "Geology," *Encyclopedia Britannica* (1956), p. 168. Quoted in *The Genesis Flood* by Henry M. Morris and John C. Whitcomb (Philadelphia: Presbyterian & Reformed Publishing Co., 1965), p. 135.

With the rise of skepticism and frank modernism, the miraculous elements of the Scriptures were increasingly denied, and the geologist's apostate theology began to affect his interpretation of geological formations. The worldwide flood concept was replaced by the theory of a local flood in the Mesopotamian area, and it is claimed that all geological formations were laid down under fairly uniform rather than very calamitous conditions. Everything, they say, can be accounted for by conditions as we find them today. This is the *uniformitarian* view. It is almost universally held by geologists who are agnostic, or who are modernistic or neo-orthodox in theology.

The diagram of a small vertebrate animal, falling to the bottom of a pond and becoming fossilized, found in many high school and college texts, exemplifies this view, but is highly erroneous, as will become clear.

The evidence against the uniformitarian view is considerable. We find no floods that compare with those responsible for laying down sedimentary deposits of the depth found in the earth; only a great flood of the proportions described in Genesis with the volcanic eruptions and flows that accompanied it and succeding lesser floods, could have done so. Sedimentary deposits nearly four-thousand feet thick have been discovered in the Buckeye Range of the Horlick Mountains on the Antarctic Continent.[4] Nor do we find any coal in formation today. None of our peat bogs, which are actually quite thin compared to the huge subterranean coal seams, show any grading into coal in their lowest depths. Nor do we find the great forces of uplift which brought forth chains of mountains, nor volcanic activity of the scope which brought forth majestic Mt. Rainier in Washington, Mt. Fujiyama in Japan, and Mt. Etna in Sicily. When a mound of a few hundred feet is formed by lava eruptions today, it makes headlines. Very important is the fact that we find little fossil formation today, whereas fossil-bearing rocks show organisms deposited very thickly in their strata. Clearly these favor catastrophism, as we shall see when discussing fossil formation.

A second weakness of the uniformitarian view is the assumption that the layers of sedimentary rocks were laid down uniformly over long periods of time, with the most primitive or ancient fossils in the lower strata and the more complex or recent fossils in the upper. But many areas do not follow this pattern, and present a

---

4. William E. Long, "Sedimentary Rocks of the Buckeye Range, Horlick Mountains, Antarctica." *Science*, 136:319-321.

formidable difficulty for this view. The explanation is that catostrophies could account for local exceptions, but the area in the Rocky Mountains which exemplifies this is very large indeed, stretching southward from southern Alberta for five hundred miles through all of Glacier National Park and including such lofty peaks as Chief Mountain and Stony Squaw Mountain. (See figs. 14, 15.) This area is approximately the size of Nova Scotia.[5]

The mountains consist largely of precambrian limestone estimated to be a billion or more years in age, while the underlying Cretaceous shale is thought to be only two hundred million years old. The geologist explains this by "thrust-faults," in which the higher side of a fault moves sideways over the lower side. The upper layer then erodes away, leaving the "older" stratum from the high side overlying the top or "younger" layer from the lower side. Considering the size of Chief Mountain, for example, this assumes both a fault and a lateral thrust of tremendous proportions. This in itself would contradict the uniformitarian view. However, there is no evidence to support a thrust-fault of such magnitude (small ones are present in some layers). Nor is there any large mass of broken rock which would have been produced in front of such a thrust. Further, there is no substantial fragmentation in the shale beneath to justify this explanation. The nonconforming areas in the Swiss Alps are even more complex and difficult to explain.

A third difficulty in the uniformitarian view is the assumption that emissions of radioactive elements are constant and the conclusion that radioactive dating is valid. This argument is treated in detail in chapter 14.

Fortunately, there is evidence of increasing disillusionment with the uniformitarian view. According to *Newsweek*:

> But now many geologists believe the counter-attack [against catastrophism] may have been all too vigorous. In their haste to reject the hand of God, they have passed over some solid evidence that could help improve their understanding of geology and evolution. . . .
>
> There is evidence, for example, that great expanses have been inundated within a matter of days. . . .[6]

Lee Bertin agrees, stating, "It must be admitted that [earth] movements in the past must have been very different from those of the

---

5. Alfred M. Rehwinkel, *The Flood* (St. Louis: Concordia Publishing House, 1951), p. 273.
6. December 23, 1963.

Figs. 14 and 15. Both Chief Mountain (above) in Glacier National Park and Stony Squaw Mountain near Banff, Alberta, are part of a formation in which Algonkian limestone overlies Cretaceous shale, something which embarrasses evolutionary geologists, who insist for other reasons that the limestone is older than the shale. To explain this phenomenon, they call this formation the "Lewis Overthrust." (Courtesy of B. Willis, U.S. Geological Survey; and Field Museum of Natural History.)

present day, and that it is debatable how far these events can be accurately reconstructed from the present day."[7] George G. Simpson, prominent evolutionist, concurs also: "Some processes (those of vulcanism and glaciation, for example) have evidently acted in the past with scales and rates that cannot by any stretch be called 'the same' or even 'approximately the same' as those of today."[8]

Norman Newell, paleontologist at the American Museum of Natural History, explains this in more detail:

> Geology students are taught that the "present is the key to the past," and they too often take it to mean that nothing ever happened that isn't happening now. But since the end of World War II, when a new generation moved in, we have gathered more data and we have begun to realize that there were many catastrophic events in the past, some of which happened just once. . . . The most recent disaster took place on the North American continent some 7,000 years ago . . . **Within perhaps only a few years,** fully three-fourths of all the large, plant-eating mammal life on the continent became extinct — camels, wooly mammoths, mastodons, ground sloths all disappeared.[9] (Emphasis mine.)

Not only are catastrophic events of the past — catastrophes of tremendous proportions — now receiving more recognition, but so is one great cataclysm — sudden in nature — which caused the extermination of many large animals only a few thousand years ago.

Norman Berrill also reports that remains of the giant sloth with a radiocarbon age of ten thousand to eleven thousand years have been found from Patagonia to as far north as Nevada, which was then "more humid, with thick forests and semitropical undergrowth. *Then something happened,* and men may have been victims as well as the beasts."[10] (Emphasis mine.) When we discuss the limitations of radiocarbon dating, we shall see that even this estimate of time is too high, and that of Newell is more nearly correct.

Alfred Romer also contends that ". . . a number of large animals which inhabited North America during the Pleistocene . . . disappeared, *apparently quite suddenly.* . . . Ground sloths, glypto-

---

7. *The Larousse Encyclopedia of the Earth* (New York: Prometheus Press), p. 197. Quoted in *Journal of the American Scientific Affiliation* (March, 1971), p. 22.

8. *This View of Life* (New York: Harcourt, Brace and World, 1964), p. 132.

9. Quoted in "God, Man and Geology," *Newsweek* (December 23, 1963), p. 48.

10. *Inherit the Earth* (New York: Dodd, 1966), p. 40.

dents, giant armadillos, camels, mastodons and mammoths all roamed this continent not very many thousand years ago. All are now gone."[11] (Emphasis mine.)

These writers feel that the fossil evidence for sudden, cataclysmic extinction found in Pleistocene formations can be accounted for by glaciers coming down from northern ice caps, possibly aided by human hunters slaying these giant animals in large numbers, but this explanation will need to be modified. There is much evidence that man did not hunt large animals other than the mammoth and the bison to any great extent. Also Rehwinkel has shown that the "glacial drift" in many areas does not show evidence of true glacial origin, despite the fact that melting and flowing ice was probably involved secondarily at times, because: (1) glaciers do not flow up hills and mountains, as would be necessary to explain some formations by this method; (2) the sorting of sedimentary deposits into different constituents points to flowing water rather than flowing ice for their origin; (3) the presence of well-preserved fossils argues for waterborne sediment rather than the violent grinding forces in a glacier.[12] This brings us to strong evidence for the Genesis flood, and the other violent upheavals, earthquakes, and volcanism that accompanied and followed it.

A recent discussion of uniformitarianism and catastrophism, entitled "Reaction and Rebuttal," provided some interesting insights. William Springstead, espousing catastrophism and quoting repeatedly from modern geologists, cited evidence for late Pleistocene extinction like that described above[13]. In rebuttal, Roger Cuffey of Pennsylvania State University, upholding the evolutionist view, stubbornly refused to acknowledge that such extinction is now widely recognized. He failed to give one solid quotation for his defense, presenting some which indicated that evidence for extinction is also found in other formations (which was irrelevant), and that the magnitude of Pleistocene extinction has been exaggerated. His statement that "even . . . a brief world-wide flood would leave unmistakable evidence from which uniformitarian principles would correctly interpret the actual historical event"[14] is meaningless,

11. *The Procession of Life* (Cleveland: World Publishing Co., 1968), pp. 254f.
12. *The Flood*, pp. 324-27.
13. "The Dying of the Giants," *Journal of the American Scientific Affiliation* (March, 1971), p. 22.
14. "Adam and Anthropology," *Journal of the American Scientific Affiliation* (March, 1971), p. 22.

and can only be ascribed to complete surrender to his fellow geologists of the evolutionist school, particularly his instructors in years past. He does not seem to be able to take issue with them in any of his writings that I have examined to date. Thus it would seem that Roger Cuffey, and others of the Mixter school of thought, have been not only too quick to swallow the claims of the uniformitarians of the past, but also, now that the pendulum is swinging, too slow in relinquishing them. This does not engender confidence in them as sound leaders in the field.

Astronomy and the Earth's Age

Some of the distant galaxies are a few billion light years away from the earth. It follows logically, many claim, that it has taken light this long to reach the earth and that the billions of years ascribed to the earth's age are therefore certain. However, a more plausible conclusion exists; when the Lord said, "Let there be light" (Gen. 1:3), He not only set luminous spheres in the heavens but simultaneously created the entire system of lights with their beams (photons) extending throughout space, so that one on earth could have detected distant heavenly bodies immediately. This will be discussed in more detail under theistic evolution.

Erosion and the Earth's Age

A friend who is uniformitarian but not evolutionary in his view (a seeming inconsistency) once remarked to me that the Grand Canyon of the Colorado River in Arizona was produced entirely by erosion. He said there is no evidence of faulting. That would please his fellow uniformitarians who favor evolution. The Grand Canyon is thought to be the most spectacular example of erosion on the continent and, inasmuch as the mile-deep canyon cuts down below the lowest strata of rock to contain fossils, it is a graphic museum of many geological processes, past and present. The evolutionist is quick to point out how long it must have taken to wear through a mile of sedimentary rock layers and cites this as evidence for the great antiquity he ascribes to the earth.

However, there is no proof that the forces of erosion have been constant in centuries past. More important, there is considerable evidence that erosion has been not the only factor and perhaps not even the most important one in forming the canyon. When I visited the canyon, I was struck by several outstanding features.

First, upon approaching the south rim from the entrance, one drives over a series of regularly spaced, rippling hills, parallel to the canyon. This is precisely what one would expect to find along the margin of a fault (a natural cleavage in the earth) of gigantic size as shown in figure 16.

This is illustrated graphically in an article by Lincoln Barnett on the forces that shaped the landscape of the earth.[15] This article is strongly dogmatic in favor of evolution and is accompanied by several paintings to show these forces at work shows a gigantic fault line with rippling hills where the fault caused the wrinkling of the earth's surface, exactly as in figure 16. It is almost as though the artist had painted his picture with the Grand Canyon in mind. This conclusion meshes well with the fact that the north rim is 1,200 feet higher than the south rim, for a fault produces an elevation of one rim and a lowering of the other.

But, one might ask, if such great forces have been at work in this area, should not one find evidence of minor faults that have resulted from them? In answer to this, we can give positive evidence. Many of us have explored the canyon from the south rim, walking down the Kaibab Trail to Phantom Ranch at the bottom, and returning to the top over Bright Angel Trail. On both of these trails, we find signs erected by the Park Service pointing to clear evidences of faulting within the canyon wall. Another sign points to buckling in the layers associated ordinarily with mountain form-

15. "The Face of the Land," *Life* (April 13, 1953), p. 92.

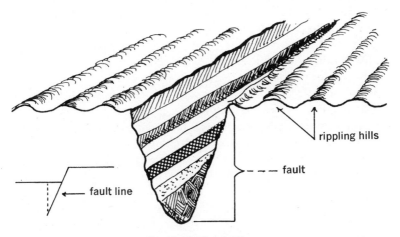

Fig. 16. Massive faulting

ing processes. It is reasonable to conclude, therefore, that faulting can account for most of the depth of the canyon, and that this force has been augmented by erosion.

Finally, despite the trumpeting of the evolutionist that the Grand Canyon is an outstanding exhibit of evolutionary change, he should be disenchanted to find that the lowest fossil-bearing rocks (Tapeats Sandstone) exhibit fossils of very complex arthropods rather than merely simple plants and animals.

9

The Fossil Record

The Formation of Fossils

A final question confronting the uniformitarian is, "How do I account for fossil-bearing deposits on the basis of uniformitarianism?" One of the first principles in paleobotany is that fossils are laid down only under special conditions — the organism in question must be covered by deposit *quickly and completely* or decay will set in and destroy the structures before fossilization can occur. For this reason fossil formation today is rare. A lava flow ordinarily destroys any plant or animal remains in its path by its intense heat. Therefore, igneous rocks are usually devoid of fossils; in rare instances lava casts have formed when the flow arrived at trees just at the point of cooling, leaving charred trunks. Metamorphic rocks have been so altered by pressure and heat that they, too, contain no fossils. The overwhelming preponderance of fossils is found in sedimentary rock, and most of these have been laid down under flood waters. In some instances they have been laid down under wind-blown loess (silt) or airborne volcanic dust. These all constitute catastrophes of the greatest dimension. Of these, only airborne volcanic dust can be said to parallel modern conditions. As already indicated, some of these sedimentary deposits are hundreds of feet thick, and bear silent testimony to flood conditions far surpassing anything modern man has every seen. Not only were the flood waters beyond our conception in magnitude, but the plants and animals entrapped were found in large quantities and buried alive. Hugh Miller, describing fossils of fish found over an area of ten thousand square miles in Scotland, comments that the remains bear "unequivocally the marks of violent death. The figures are contorted, contracted, curved, the tail in many instances is bent around to the head, the spines stuck out, the fins are spread to the 'full' as fish who were dying as earth sediment, stirred up from the surface of the continents by the Flood, settled thicker and heavier upon them."[1]

One quite naturally and logically thinks of the flood of Noah's time as the cause of these formations. A slowly rising flood of worldwide proportions would explain many things. As the land animals would be able to keep climbing to higher elevations, we would expect to find them more often in the upper strata, and marine animals in the lower. Further, as they would be increasingly concentrated in a smaller area, we can account for the hordes of bones found in certain local deposits; a rock in the museum of Princeton University is crowded thick with bone parts from nine rhinoceros' heads.

Extinct and Modern Species

We often find fossils of extinct animals and present-day species together in the same rock formation. The museum at Scotts Bluff National Monument in western Nebraska once exhibited fossils of a "modern" beaver and of an extinct mountain beaver twice as large. (I understand these are now in the University Museum in Lincoln.) Since these were found in the same formation, the conclusion is obvious; they were contemporary, and the modern beaver has continued unchanged while the mountain beaver became extinct. Had the modern beaver been found in a layer above the mountain beaver, however, the evolutionist would have claimed evidence of evolutionary descent from the mountain beaver to our present form. Had the modern beaver been found in a lower layer, and we frequently find examples of this kind, he would admit a contemporary existence again, or speculate that one layer had slid up over the top of the other. Inasmuch as they are together, he

---

1. Hugh Miller, *The Old Red Sandstone*, p. 221. Quoted in *After Its Kind*, pp. 75f.

freely admits (indeed, he is forced to) that they were contemporaries. We can account for all fossils in this manner; the modern species have continued unchanged and the others have become extinct, *leaving no evidence whatever that they were gradually changed into another species.*

Extinct Species and Man

We have conclusive evidence that man has encountered plants and animals in times past, in the live state, which are now extinct. In caves of the Pyrenees Mountains of France and Spain we find drawings of mammoths and other now-extinct species. Mammoths have been found frozen in Siberia and Alaska with much of the skin and flesh intact. It is said that Emperor Ivan the Terrible of Russia dined on mastodon steak, a rare serving indeed! One from Alaska is on exhibit in a glass-covered, frozen chest in the American Museum of Natural History in New York City (fig. 17).

Romain Robert, then president of the Prehistoric Society of the Ariege Department, France, found in a "new" cave drawings of sixty-one mammoths, twelve bison, eight goats, six horses, and four rhinoceros. The mammoth, among others shown, has long been extinct, yet the artisans who drew these likenesses *saw* them. Far from being crude drawings, Robert describes them as being "among the most beautiful specimens of prehistoric art yet discovered."[2] (See figs. 18-20.)

At times footprints of man have been found in the same rock formations as these animals. Literally dozens, perhaps hundreds of species of birds and mammals have become extinct during historic times. In Europe the wild cow and horse both became extinct a few centuries ago; in Asia the dromedary camel has been extinct, in the wild state, for generations. On this continent the giant mink, the eastern elk, the Carolina paroquet, the Eskimo curlew, the Arctic auk, and the passenger pigeon have become extinct in recent times. Some living today can still remember the passenger pigeon, the last of which died in the Cincinnati zoo in 1914. Within my memory, the last heath hen died on Martha's Vineyard in 1932. For some of these we have fossils in sedimentary formations, *yet they have never developed into anything else.*

The best explanation appears to be that the great bulk of fossils today were produced at the time of the flood and that the process

---

2. *Time* (August 6, 1954), p. 42.

of extinction began immediately thereafter. Many of the largest land animals may well have perished soon after; it seems almost the rule that survival becomes difficult for any species that has been reduced to a few individuals.

Some of these were undoubtedly killed off by man himself. Paul S. Martin of the University of Arizona's geochronology laboratories, commenting on the extinction of "71 percent of the large Pleistocene mammals on this continent," states: "The fossil record indi-

Fig. 17. Frozen ground in Alaska yielded this well-preserved baby woolly mammoth, now on exhibit in a glass-covered, frozen chest in the American Museum of Natural History, New York City. (Courtesy of American Museum of Natural History.)

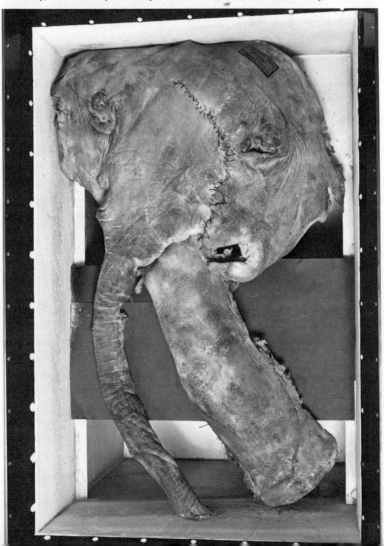

Figs. 18 and 19. Cave paintings (here reproduced by R. Cassein) of the now-extinct bison (above) and woolly rhinoceros demonstrate both that man was once contemporaneous with these animals and that prehistoric man was capable of very refined art. Both paintings were discovered in France. (Courtesy of Field Museum of Natural History.)

cates it coincided with and was triggered by the arrival here of the prehistoric hunters who once fluted points and spread their culture from coast to coast. . . ."[3]

3. *Nature*, 212:319. Quoted in *Dateline In Science* (December 2, 1966).

Fig. 20. Another product of prehistoric art is the sculpture of a fighting ibex, discovered in Gargas Cave in southern France. Its fine proportions and musculature demonstrate further the high level of prehistoric man's culture. (Courtesy of Field Museum of Natural History.)

There is reason to believe, further, that man coexisted with the huge reptiles which have long been extinct. *The Genesis Flood*, by Whitcomb and Morris, presents a photograph of a dinosaur track and a human footprint, cut from the same Cretaceous limestone formation near Glen Rose, Texas, despite the fact that dinosaurs supposedly became extinct seventy million years before man appeared.[4] Human footprints also have been found in carboniferous rocks estimated to be 250 million years old.

These have been found in many states, from the Rocky Mountains eastward to Pennsylvania and Virginia. Albert Ingalls, who has photographed some of these prints (which varied in length from five to ten inches), describes this wide range of occurrence where they " have been found in the surface of exposed rocks, and more and more keep turning up as the years go by."[5]

---

4. P. 174.
5. "The Carboniferous Mystery," *Scientific American*, 162 (January, 1960), p. 14. Quoted in *The Genesis Flood*, pp. 172f.

"Living Fossils"

The fossil record's impact on my thinking was crucial. Like most beginning university students, I was rather naive and was gradually carried along with the mainstream, accepting the "facts" of evolution as they were subtly propounded in lectures and textbooks. However, I began studying a booklet given to me by a Christian friend. This booklet dealt with the question of fossils and what they really prove. I was amazed to learn that many fossils of plants and animals are exactly like their counterparts today and that, through all the time that has elapsed since their deposition as fossils, they have shown no trace of evolution! This arrested my thinking and shook me to the very foundation. I became wiser in my evaluation of the teaching that I received; I became convinced of the biblical account of creation, although I was not converted to the Christian faith until a year later.

Since that time, rock collecting — and especially fossil collecting — has become a fascinating hobby, and I have found many fossils just like modern plants and animals (fig. 21). I have specimens of amber washed up on the shores of the Baltic Sea which demonstrate beautifully the structures of a spider, an ant, and several gnats (fig. 22). Every vein in their wings, every hair on the legs and feet, every detail on their antennae can be seen, and they are just like our species today. I have climbed Peterson's Butte near Lebanon, Oregon, to find fossils of clams, razor clams, and snails that are mirror images of our modern species, and I continue to add examples like these to my collection as opportunity affords.

Literally hundreds of species living today have been found in nearly perfect preservation as fossils, some so deep in the earth that they are called, even by the skeptics, "living fossils." One example is the lungfish, species of which are found in Africa, Australia, and South America. It is able to breathe with gills while in water and from an air bladder while out of the water. Curiously, it forms a "cocoon" of mud and mucus when its pond dries up and lives on stored fat. It is found in rocks estimated to be 300,000 years old.

Other examples of "living fossils" (with their supposed fossil ages, in some instances) are, to name a few: the opossum, several species of spiders, all of the snow-fleas, the platypus (50 million years), the echidna (50 million years), the horseshoe crab (190 million years), the coelacanth (almost 300 million years), some species of snails (300 million years), several species of cockroaches (350 million years).

Fig. 21. These fossil remains from Cretaceous rock are virtually identical with their modern counterparts: persimmon (below), buckthorn (1 above), elm (2 above), poplar (3 above), and sycamore. (Courtesy of Field Museum of Natural History.)

Fig. 22. Fossils of this quality can be studied in detail and their identity with modern species confirmed. The insects on the left are in amber, permitting examination of the antennae, hairs on the legs, and veins of the wings. The insect below is a dragonfly. (Courtesy of Field Museum of Natural History [left] and American Museum of Natural History.)

The Geological Timetable

We have indicated that the lowest fossil-bearing rocks of the "Cambrian period" found in the Grand Canyon contain complex animal forms. This has been true consistently in the deepest rocks found. As Dr. Austin H. Clark of the Smithsonian Institute stated:

> So we see that the fossil record, the actual history of the animal life on the earth, bears out the assumption that at its very first appearance animal life in its broader features was in essentially the same form as that in which we now know it. . . . Thus, so far as concerns the major groups of animals, the creationists seem to have the better of the argument. There is not the slightest evidence that any of the major groups arose from any other.[6]

A. H. Cook wrote in similar vein and with equal certainty:

> The first undisputed traces of animal life which appear in the Cambrian epoch exhibit the same phyletic distinctions as now exist: sponges, echinoderms, mollusca, and worms, formed already in those immeasurably remote ages, groups apparently as generally distinct from one another as they are at the present time.[7]

The sudden appearance of these complex animals, without forerunners in the fossil record, is a striking and dramatic evidence of special creation:

> Both the sudden appearance and the remarkable composition of the animal life characteristic of Cambrium times are sometimes explained away or overlooked by biologists. Yet recent paleontological research has made the puzzle of this sudden proliferation of living organisms increasingly difficult for anyone to evade. The strata of Cambrium age, however, contain fossils of a remarkably varied array of multicellular animals.
>
> These animals were neither primitive nor generalized in anatomy: they were complex organisms that clearly belonged to the various distinct phyla or major groups of animals. . . .
>
> Yet before the Cambrian there is scarcely a trace of them. The appearance of the Lower Cambrian fauna . . . can reasonably be called a "sudden" event.
>
> One can no longer dismiss this event by assuming that all Pre-Cambrian rocks have been too greatly altered by time to allow the fossils ancestral to the Cambrian metazoans to be preserved . . .[8]

---

6. *Quarterly Review of Biology* (December, 1928), p. 539. Quoted in *Modern Science and Christian Faith* (Wheaton: Van Kampen Press, 1948), p. 44.
7. *Cambridge Natural History,* p. 5.
8. *Science Digest* (March, 1968) pp. 50f.

Even in rocks estimated (by the evolutionist) to be one billion years old, we still find contemporary species. Examination of rocks from central Australia, Michigan, and Montana, through the electron microscope, has revealed fossils that were "indistinguishable from some present types of algae. Over the last billion years, Baarghorn and Schopf feel, they may have remained unchanged by evolution."[9]

A very recent testimony from professor Adolph Portmann is in complete harmony with these conclusions:

> A study of this subject leads . . . back to the oldest known rocks [those of the Cambrian period], which were formed under the sea: but even these can give us no explanation of the origins and development of the higher animals, for the animal world of the Cambrian period already contained numerous snails, mussels, cephalopods, and marine arthropods and echinoderms . . . The source of life appears to be an eternally hidden secret.[10]

Do not fail to grasp the significance of this generous admission by scientists who are obviously not believers in special creation. The deepest fossil-bearing rock known shows no drawing together of the various forms of plants and animals; they were still as far apart and different from one another as in the highest or "youngest" strata, and are comparable to marine forms existing today. The reason for this, however, is a "hidden secret" only to those who have turned away from the one source that has proven reliable in explaining man's origin, nature and destiny: the Word of God. This will be discussed in a later chapter.

Transitional Forms

Evolutionists have been trying for years to find fossil evidence that lungfish gradually graded into amphibia and that winged reptiles evolved into birds, but their search has been fruitless. They have speculated that the bat stems originally from wingless, furry creatures like shrews, but there are no intermediate forms to bear this out.

It has been often asserted that the horse developed from a small, three-toed form, and some even say from a five-toed form before that. Most of these fossils of horses and their supposed ancestors

9. W. B. Marland and Martin J. S. Rudwick, "The Great Infra-Cambrian Ice Age," *Scientific American* (August, 1964), pp. 34-36.
10. "The Significance of Oceanography Today," *Nautilus*, No. 2 (Basle: J. R. Geigy, S.A., 1966), p. 1.

have come from surface formations in locations far from one another rather than from successive layers above one another, leaving no evidence that one evolved from another. Byron Nelson calls attention to the fact that, according to the evolutionist, the horse should pass through a five-toed stage in its embryological development; but it does not, indicating that either the theory of comparative embryology or that of paleontology — or both — is in error. The same is true for the alleged evolution of the elephant.

More conclusively, Stuart E. Nevins has studied the stratum called the Rattlesnake Formation of the John Day Country in Oregon, where both *Neohipparion* (a three-toed grazing animal which is supposedly in the ancestral line of the horse) and *Pilohippus* (a "one-toed," very horse-like animal) are found in the same stratum (layer). He concludes that *"No transition between the three-toed and the single hoofed forms has been found!"* (Emphasis his.) Again, he aptly states that "one wonders if some other explanation [than evolution] might be more plausible."[11]

In summary, the fossil record shows:

1. Evidence of great catastrophes — huge floods, volcanic eruptions and lava flows, massive glaciation, large meteors falling.

2. Sediments from flood waters comprise the largest mass of the earth's crust.

3. The sudden emergence of all major groups, which are as much unlike each other as they are now and some specimens of which are virtually the same as modern species.

4. Absence of transitional forms necessary to prove evolution.

5. Sudden extinction of large land animals by some great catastrophes, such as the great flood and the events which followed it.

6. Evidence of abnormal conditions in the past, such as tropical vegetation in the frozen Arctic.

Geologists' Guesses

One "link" that was long prized by the evolutionist was a large fish called the coelacanth (fig. 23). It had fleshy fins which, it was fancied, developed into legs when the fish decided to come ashore for a terrestrial existence. One such coelacanth fossil was found in the excavation for a library on the Princeton University campus. Such fossils were dated back to 160 million years, and it was calculated to have become extinct about 90 million years ago.

---

11. "Post-Flood Strata of the John Day Country, Northeastern Oregon," *Creation Research Society Quarterly*, 10 (March, 1974), p. 196.

Imagine the sensation created when, in 1952, a fisherman between Madagascar and Mozambique pulled in a heavy, five-foot coelacanth, flopping and very much alive! Since that time, other specimens have been caught near this site.

As the science of oceanography has expanded and intensified, other species thought to be long extinct have been found living at great depths. Adolph Portmann of the Zoological Institute at the University of Basel comments: "There was universal amazement when the first major explorations of the ocean depths revealed that at depths of thousands of meters organisms were still living which had been regarded as long since dead and gone. These included the rare stalked sea lilies or crinoids, relatives of the starfish and sea urchins, as well as many types of crabs which had been thought to be extinct since the Mesozoic period in the earth."[12] He also reports the discovery of a snail-like mollusk at a depth of nearly 12,000 feet and other mollusks and worm-like creatures, formerly known only in fossils, at depths which supposedly would

12. "The Significance of Oceanography Today," No. 2, p. 1.

Fig. 23. When the coelacanth had been found only in fossil form, evolutionists concluded it had evolved into a higher form and become extinct ninety million years ago. But in 1952 a man fishing in the Indian Ocean caught one, creating a worldwide sensation. (Courtesy of American Museum of Natural History.)

not support life. Some now think that we may yet find trilobites, thought to be extinct for 300 million years.[13]

A similar report by Columbia University scientists appeared in *Science News Letter*: "Believed extinct for 300,000,000 years, four little snail-like creatures have been dredged up from the depths of the Pacific Ocean. . . . The specimens were caught in nets at a depth of more than 3 miles . . . west of Lima, Peru. . . . The tiny sea creature has changed little from its ancestors of the Cambrian period."[14]

The process of coal formation also has been poorly understood by geologists. For years it was taught that coal was formed by great heat and pressure. The latter was felt necessary presumably because many fossils in coal beds are *flattened*, carbonized remnants of plants. However, pressure may not be necessary, as evidenced by the following account: "My brother and I were digging coal from a side hill mine in Montana. We had moved a six-foot layer of earth off the coal vein and dug deeply into the coal when we began to uncover a perfect tree trunk with limbs, knots, branches, and even

---

13. *Nautilus*, No. 1, p. 1.
14. (Dec. 27, 1958). Reprinted by permission.

Fig. 24. This bark of a "scale tree" (Sigillaria pennsylvanian) contradicts the long-standing theory that great pressure is essential to the formation of coal. (Courtesy of Field Museum of Natural History.)

leaves, *turned into a fine grade of coal* that could be lighted with a match, perfectly preserved in the coal seam."[15]

The Field Museum of Natural History in Chicago has on display a fine specimen of coal formation much like the one described above. It is a large stump with roots, very much in the round and unflattened, but completely converted into coal (fig. 24).

Some of the most artful guessing, however, has been reserved for the fossil remains of man, to which we shall now turn our attention.

---

15. Kenneth Anderson, "Strange Things About Trees," *American Forests* (August, 1956).

10

Anthropology

Prehistoric Men

Some years ago, the "Hall of Man" was one of the most impressive displays of Chicago's Field Museum. Here one could see many "restorations" of "prehistoric man." In addition to glass-enclosed displays of the artist's conception of primitive races of men, there were life-sized statues in the hall, some with large, fang-like canine teeth, some with glazed, ape-like eyes and thick facial hair, one with a wild pig thrown over his shoulder. Their arrangement showed a gradual progression from the ape-like Java man to the more intelligent looking Cro-Magnon at the other end of the spectrum. They were almost lifelike enough to reach out and touch you. Since this was the work of men who specialized in anthropology and paleontology, one gained the impression that these statues represented the best and most authoritative scientific study. Doubtless thousands of visitors from all over the world, in filing through the halls past the grimacing statues of Heidelberg man, Java man, Piltdown man, Neanderthal man, and Cro-Magnon got the impression that these proved beyond any reasonable doubt the evolutionary development of man from lower animals (fig. 25).

But, upon what evidence were these restorations based? I later

Fig. 25. These reconstructions of Java man (upper left), Piltdown man (upper right), Neanderthal man (lower left), and Heidelberg man, all produced by J. H. McGregor, may impress the uninitiated, but they are plainly imaginary. (Courtesy of American Museum of Natural History.)

found that the scientists had drawn sweeping conclusions from very fragmentary "evidence," which we will now consider.

Heidelberg Man

This restoration is based entirely on a single lower jawbone with its teeth, which are now conceded to be distinctly human.[1] It was found near Maurer, Germany, in 1907. The man was giant in size, but there is no reason to doubt that he was human in every way.

Java Man (Pithecanthropus erectus)

The only remains from this creature were the top of a skull, a thigh bone (femur), and a tooth, found by Dubois in 1891 along the bank of a river in Java. There are considerable reasons to question whether the bones, however, even belong to the same individual. Dubois himslf claimed to have found the skull portion about three feet from where he had found the tooth a month earlier. Worse still, he claims the thigh bone was found a year later and fifty feet away. Further, the tooth was found with two others that were proven to be those of an orangutan. The skull contour is not remarkable and is thought by some (including Dr. Albert Churchward) to be that of a pigmy. The fragment lacks all of the facial area, including both jaws. What fragmentary evidence on which to "reconstruct" the rest of the body! To prepare a restoration with features partly ape-like and partly human on such "evidence" does not commend itself to those seeking real scientific evidence.

Since Dubois' time, G.H.R. Von Koenigswald carried on additional excavations in Java, finding another skull cap and a lower jaw, which were considered to belong to the same species. Von Koenigswald believed the Java man, however, to be not intermediate between apes and men but fully human, in part because stone hatchets and other implements were found nearby.[2] This is the view of W. M. Krogman, University of Pennsylvania anthropologist, who said: "Concerning Peking man, Java man, and Piltdown man, 'The first two are related to each other and are definitely human.' "[3] In all, it is claimed that remains from at least six

1. R. A. Stirton, *Time, Life and Man* (New York: John Wiley & Sons, 1963), p. 516.
2. Edwin D. Neff, "Our Forgotten Superman," *Nature* (November, 1948), pp. 470f.
3. W. M. Krogman, "Man," *World Book Encyclopedia,* (Chicago: Field Enterprises, 1951), p. 4747.

individuals have been found, establishing it as a distinct race, but these are so incomplete as to raise doubts. Some scientists have felt that Peking man (*Sinanthropus pekinesis*), whose remains disappeared with Communist advance in China, and remains found at Ternifine, Algeria, are relatives of Java man; but the fragments from Algeria are too incomplete for anything but speculation. William Straus, anthropologist at Johns Hopkins University, comments:

> Were Pithecanthropines present in North Africa in middle Pleistocene times? On the basis of the Ternifine mandibles, this appears likely, but not certain. For it must be realized that neither jaws alone, nor teeth alone, nor jaws plus teeth alone, can with assurance make the man — no more than braincase alone or face alone. Of this we now have ample testimony in the "suspense list" of paleoanthropology — from Hong Kong, from Sangiran, from Kanam, from Kanjers, from Heidelberg, from Swanscombe, from Fontechevade. Suspended judgment is the greatest triumph of intellectual discipline.[4]

Peking Man

Near Peking, China, the remains of forty skeletons have been found, some nearly complete, some fragmentary. The brain size was that of the Negritos living today. Peking men used fire and fashioned choppers and scrapers from bone, stone, and antlers. They were true men. Their remains disappeared when the Chinese Communists' advance overwhelmed the area where the paleontologists had been working, and they have not been seen since by Western scientists.

Piltdown Man (Eoanthropus dawsoni)

These remains were found by an English lawyer named Dawson in a gravel pit in England from 1908 to 1911, without accurate measurement of the site to ascertain whether they belonged to the same individual. Inasmuch as there were four skull fragments, part of a mandible (jawbone), a tooth, and a flint, some felt this specimen rested on a somewhat surer footing than the first two "apemen" mentioned. It was pictured in most textbooks of paleontology, and casts or "restorations" of it were found in large museums throughout the world.

---

4. William L. Straus, Jr., "Pithecanthropus in Africa?" *Science*, 123 (March 23, 1956), p. 498.

Yet, this find was surrounded with more uncertainty than any of the others. The four skull bones were very incomplete and lent themselves to considerable speculation, as the "restorer" could fit them together according to his own bias. Thus, Dr. Smith-Woodword estimated the brain capacity at 1070cc, which is subhuman or nearly so, whereas Sir Arthur Keith, also an evolutionist, estimated it to be 1500cc, which is within normal human skull limits.[5] Furthermore, several eminent authorities were convinced that the jawbone belonged to a chimpanzee. The climax came in 1953, however, when Dr. K. P. Oakley of the British Museum and professors W. E. LeGros Clark, and J. S. Weiner of Oxford University blasted the case for Piltdown man once for all, showing not only that the jaw portion was that of a chimpanzee, but also that the jawbone had been retouched and stained and the teeth filed to give the appearance of antiquity.[6] Piltdown man, scientists agreed, was the greatest anthropological hoax of the century, and it was quietly withdrawn from textbooks and museum cases.

The effects of this hoax were far-reaching. This was apparent on a recent revisit to the Field Museum of Natural History. No longer do "ape-men" statues line the hall to amaze and perplex the public. Piltdown man can be found nowhere; Heidelberg man has been rightly reduced to the "Heidelberg jaw" and is retired to an inconspicuous side case. More emphasis is given to the remains of modern man, which are based on firmer evidence.

One science writer, on reviewing the calamity that had befallen Piltdown man, was quick to admit that Java man also might have to be given up by the evolutionist because the evidence supporting it was so fragmentary, and that it was now wise to concentrate on newer finds in Africa, which we will discuss later.

While the first four "ape-men" are based on very flimsy evidence, the next two have rather complete skull remains, making them far more authentic.

Neanderthal Man

The first skeletons of this race of men were found in the Neander Valley in Germany in 1856. Since then other skeletons have been found in other parts of Europe, as well as in Asia and Africa. The skull is characterized by heavy frontal (brow) ridges, strong jaws,

---

5. *Nature* (October 16, 1913). Includes sketches of the "brain capacities."
6. "Monkey Business: Piltdown Man," *Scientific American*, 190 (January, 1954). p. 38.

and a sloping forehead. There is no reason for classifying Neanderthal man as another species *(Homo neanderthalensis)* since his brain was as large as that of modern man.

Some have claimed there were two separate strains — a progressive or "modern type," and a conservative or "primitive type," but the two are sometimes found together in the same cave; the distinction is apparently an artificial one that does not take into account normal variability.

A number of reasons exist why this man should be considered neither ape-like nor somewhere between the apes and man. Dr. Carleton S. Coon, University of Pennsylvania anthropologist, points out that he had a higher material culture than some twentieth century primitive tribes; he made superior stone tools, was skilled as a hunter, and apparently demonstrated "good verbal communication."[7] He used paint and had many uses for flint.[8] D. T. Dale Stewart of the Smithsonian Institute relates that a Neanderthal skeleton found at Shanidor, Iraq, had undergone surgical amputation of an arm above the elbow.[9]

A report of the 1957 meeting of the American Association for the Advancement of Science sheds additional light on Neanderthal man: "A group of anthropologists had kind words to say for Neanderthal man . . . generally described as a dim-witted monster whose long arms dangled forward from stooping shoulders. 'This is slander,' says William L. Straus, Jr., of Johns Hopkins University. 'Neanderthal man probably stood upright with his limbs in seemly positions.' " Dr. Loren E. Eiseley of the University of Pennsylvania added that Neanderthal man did not have fangs or other wild animal features. "These unappealing characteristics were given to him by heavy-handed reconstructors."[10]

Was this a race destroyed by the great flood in Noah's time? While this is a possibility, it should be apparent that some of our present racial types, particularly the Australian aborigines and the Negritos of western New Guinea, manifest the same prominent frontal ridges and receding forehead.[11]

Seventy-two skullcaps and other human remains resembling Nean-

7. "Neanderthal Man Upgraded by Scientists," *Lancaster Intelligencer Journal,* Lancaster, Pa., (May 31, 1956).
8. Ibid.
9. Ibid.
10. *Time* (January 7, 1957), p. 38.
11. Donald F. Thompson, "An Arnhem Land Adventure," *National Geographic Magazine* (December, 1948), pp. 771-94.

derthal man have been found by Von Koenigswald in Java, and have been called Solo man, who was cannibalistic. Stirton acknowledges that "he may have been near to the ancestry of the New Guinea and Australian aborigines. Neanderthal man, Rhodesian man, and Solo man apparently are so closely related that some authorities have considered referring to them as one species."[12]

Time magazine's science editor has echoed this growing conviction concerning "the flat-nosed aborigine of Australia, with his receding forehead . . . some anthropologists, noting that his skullcap is much thicker and his brain capacity 20 percent smaller than that of European man, suggest that he is the last survivor of the primordial primates who succeeded Neanderthal man."[13]

Further, this type of skull and sturdy body build is often seen among Europeans today. According to Dr. Carleton Coon's investigation, through interbreeding, Neanderthal man left descendants who still appear today. Dr. Coon explains: "These are people with a receding brow, long face, big nose and stocky body build. But there is absolutely nothing wrong with their intelligence. It's my contention that the Neanderthal man was intelligent."[14] In short, this is an indirect concession that he was *Homo sapiens* and nothing less.

William Kornfield, visiting professor of anthropology at Wheaton College, summarizes the modern view of Neanderthal man:

> While the general skeletal and facial structure and dentition of Neanderthal appear to be more rugged than those of most modern men today, Brace (1964) says that "no one of those differences is outside the range of variation of modern man" and that "there is reason to believe that they were at least as intelligent as modern man, if not more so" (1967). . . . On the basis of his completely erect posture, a cranial capacity every bit as great as (and sometimes greater than) that of modern man, and the fact that his skeletal remains have been found in direct association with cultural artifacts and ceremonial burials, present day anthropologists now consider Neanderthal man as **Homo sapiens.**[15]

Cro-Magnon

Many fine skulls and practically complete skeletons of this racial

---

12. Stirton, *Time, Life and Man,* p. 519.
13. *Time* (June 16, 1967), p. 42.
14. "Neanderthal Man Upgraded by Scientists."
15. William J. Kornfield, "The Early-Date Genesis Man," *Christianity Today* (June 8, 1973), p. 8.

type have been found. There is little disagreement among scientists that this race is identical to the modern European, *Homo sapiens*. His culture was even more advanced than that of Neanderthal man. He was a fine craftsman, using bone and stone tools and making such things as stone and ivory statuettes. Physically, he was superior even to our generation of Europeans: *"Homo sapiens,* Cro-Magnon was somewhat taller and more muscular than his modern counterpart, with a large brain — about 1650cc — compared to modern man's average of 1350cc."[16]

His skill as an artist was demonstrated in the December, 1948, issue of *National Geographic Magazine,* in which many color photographs revealed to the public for the first time the accuracy in proportion and the fineness of shading characterizing his paintings of animals (many now extinct) in caves in the French Pyrenees Mountains.[17] The paintings compare favorably with the finest of artistry among the American Indians.

Remains of both Neanderthal and Cro-Magnon men have been found in caves with fossils of the woolly rhinoceros, a cave hyena, and extinct horses,[18] indicating that these animals were contemporary with modern man. Further, both Neanderthal and Cro-Magnon remains are occasionally found in the same caves. Apparently Cro-Magnon, with his superior culture, displaced the Neanderthal race in Europe, much as modern European culture has replaced aboriginal culture in many parts of the world today.

Recent Discoveries in Africa

Despite the trumpeting of each new find by anthropologists in Africa, little comfort can be given the evolutionist after all the evidence is sifted. The following interesting species have been discovered:

Pro-consul

A nearly complete skull of this creature was found on an island in Lake Victoria by L. S. B. Leakey. It is recognized as being clearly an ape, and shows no definitive trend in the direction of human development.

---

16. "The Discovery of Cro-Magnon Man," *MD Magazine* (August, 1968) p. 91.

17. N. Casteret, "Lascaux Cave, Cradle of World Art," *National Geographic Magazine,* 94 (December 1948), pp. 771-94.

18. Stirton, *Time, Life and Man,* p. 519.

Swartzkrans "Ape-man"

This is based entirely on a giant-sized jaw fragment found by South African paleontologist Robert Broom in a rock in Swartzkrans Cave. The nature of the face, brain case, and body are entirely the result of the discoverer's enthusiastic fabrication. The jaw fragment is so incomplete it must be regarded as inferior even to the Heidelberg jaw as evidence.

Prometheus "Ape-man"

This is based on a jaw fragment of an ape found in a cave with some charred bones of a pig and an antelope. There is no proof that "Prometheus" made the fire that charred the bones, nor that he himself may not have been eaten by the fire builder. This again "begs the question."

Australopithecus Boisei (East Africa Man)

This is based upon two remarkedly well-preserved pieces of maxillary bone (upper jaw) with teeth in place, and approximately four hundred skull pieces found by Dr. and Mrs. L. S. B. Leakey in Olduvai Gorge in Tanzania. While the teeth and jaw are remarkably human, the restored skull appears just as remarkably like an anthropoid ape with virtually no forehead (fig. 26). In fact, on close examination of the photographs available, the remains raise the same questions as those raised by remains of Java man and Piltdown man.

Inasmuch as the skull fragments were not attached to the jaw, how can we be certain that they belong to the same individual? It is stated that the skull bones were found "below" the jaw, but how far below? And over how large an area? It is known that large quantities of dirt were screened to obtain the parts fitted together; as Leakey himself reveals, "In order not to lose a single precious scrap, we had *to remove and sift tons of scree below the find.*"[19] (Emphasis mine.)

A second and obvious question is, "Does the jaw become human, while the skull remains clearly that of an anthropoid ape?" The photographs on page 422 of the article cited above, in which the restored skull of *Australopithecus* is compared with those of modern man and a gorilla, suggest that the upper part is that of an

---

19. L. S. B. Leakey, "Finding the World's Oldest Man," *National Geographic Magazine,* 118 (September, 1960), p. 443.

anthropoid ape and does not fit the apparently human jaw below, as seen in figure 27.

This is shown in several anatomical features: (1) the absence of a forehead and presence of a sagittal crest; (2) the thick periorbital bone around the eye sockets; (3) eyes at least as close together as the gorilla's, in contrast with the wide space between human eyes; (4) the upper limit of the nasal opening distinctly below the lower limit of the eye socket rather than above it and crowned with a peak as in the gorilla skull; (5) wide and broadly flared malar or cheek bones like the gorilla's.

We have reason to ask if this is a human upper jaw "restored" with the bones of an ape. This is the reverse of Piltdown man in which a "restoration" was made with the lower jaw of an ape and the skull bones of a man.

Recall that Smith-Woodward and Keith, both ardent evolutionists, disagreed sharply on the brain capacity of Piltdown man, one favoring 1070cc and the other 1500cc. If these men found it impossible to agree on how these four large bones would be placed properly in the skull, we can see the utter hopelessness of trying to fit to-

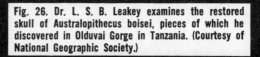

Fig. 26. Dr. L. S. B. Leakey examines the restored skull of Australopithecus boisei, pieces of which he discovered in Olduvai Gorge in Tanzania. (Courtesy of National Geographic Society.)

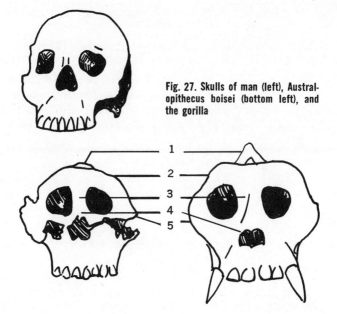

Fig. 27. Skulls of man (left), Austral-opithecus boisei (bottom left), and the gorilla

gether four hundred skull bones, many of them tiny and similarly incomplete, with any assurance of accuracy. Dr. Leakey describes the difficulty they faced back at camp: "We faced the problem of reassembly, a feat somewhat akin to putting together a complex three-dimensional jigsaw puzzle."[20]

And, we might add, he may have been working with parts of two such jigsaw puzzles, complicating the task even more.

More recently Dr. Leakey's son, Richard Leakey, discovered a skull in Kenya east of Lake Rudolph which is believed to be the same species.[21] However, either the skull was flattened by compression, or the skull proportions are much flatter than the elder Leakey envisioned. The upper jaw is so incomplete that at this time it cannot be identified in any way as pertaining to the earlier one described above. Significantly, in the report, Richard Leakey admits he no longer believes this creature to be ancestral to man, nor a user of tools.

The Chillean man skull fragments found by Dr. Leakey's expedition are unquestionably human.[22]

20. Ibid.

21. *National Geographic Magazine,* 137 (May, 1970), p. 715.

22. L.S.B. Leaky and Robert Sisson, "Exploring 1,750,000 Years into Man's Past," *National Geographic Magazine,* 120 (October, 1961), p. 581.

Many anthropologists have become skeptical of the accuracy and trustworthiness of Leakey's work. Dr. Carleton S. Coon, University of Pennsylvania anthropologist and a Leakey supporter, describes the reaction to his work in Kenya, where he attempted to show a greater antiquity for man:

> . . . a British geologist of great repute, P. G. H. Boswell, went to East Africa to study the geology of these two sites in detail. His report cast a cloud over the reliability of their dates which has never blown away. In his brief report he states that the sites had not been mapped or photographed. He was unable to find the exact spots from which the fossils had been taken.
> . . . Twenty years have passed since these events. The scientific world is still divided between Leakey's supporters, . . . and those who through honest skepticism or conflicting theories do not believe in the apparent age of these remains.[23]

European Cave Men

The Neanderthal man is sometimes called the first cave man of Europe. However, dwelling in caves does not necessarily indicate primitivism. Gypsies now dwell in caves near Granada, Spain, and exemplify modern Europeans. Further, there is no evidence that caves were the exclusive or even the regular dwelling place of Neanderthal and Cro-Magnon men. They may have used the caves principally as burial grounds, as Abraham did, or for tribal meetings or religious gatherings. They may have used them at times as a place of refuge, just as the early Christians did who "wandered in deserts, and in mountains, and in dens and caves of the earth" (Heb. 11:38), and as the Waldensians did even before the Reformation. As we have seen, the paintings on the walls and ceilings of caves in the French Pyrenees reveal that Cro-Magnon men were accomplished artists and far from primitive.

Conclusion

When all the evidence is in and all the smoke has cleared away, the "proof" for any "ape-men" consists of bone fragments so incomplete that any such classification becomes impossible. The only complete or near complete fossil skeletons, like those of Neanderthal man and Cro-Magnon, are identical with living representatives today.

---

23. Carleton S. Coon, *The Story of Man* (New York: Alfred A. Knopf, 1958), pp. 37f.

In 1884 an amateur Egyptologist, Frank S. DeHass, U. S. Consul to Palestine, examined a large number of Egyptian mummies. The mummies were so common in Egypt at that time that some were used for fuel. DeHass concluded that they were actually superior to the modern Egyptian, and that no evolutionary trend from primitive to complex could be found. These mummies were only approximately three thousand years old, but the same has been true of those which are five thousand years old. Baron Cuvier, examining the embalmed remains of animals buried in the tombs with human remains, also concluded that these were identical with modern species. If in five thousand years it is impossible to detect any change in man, it is no wonder that the evolutionist speculates in terms of millions of years.

The study of anthropology reveals many ways in which man and the apes differ markedly in structure. Beals and Hoijer, in their widely used textbook, point out nineteen differences.[24] (See fig. 28 for a summary of some of these.)

The facts all point to the conclusion which geneticist William

---

24. Ralph L. Beals and Harry Hoijer, *An Introduction to Anthropology* (New York: Macmillan Co., 1965).

STRUCTURAL CHARACTER	APES	MAN
Upper lip	Very long	Relatively short
Canine teeth	Project beyond other teeth; necessitates up-and-down chewing	Do not project — enables rotary chewing
Legs	Shorter than arms	Longer than arms
Stance	Semierect; knuckles on ground	Erect
Feet	Grasping	Weight-supporting
Brain case	500cc in gorilla; 400cc in chimpanzee	1450cc in man
Cerebrum	Moderately large	Very large — covers other two parts; large associated areas
Head hair	Scanty on chimpanzee; always straight	Varies; may be thick; may be straight but also varies from curly to kinky

Fig. 28. Comparison of the ape with man

Tinkle draws: "Man has always been a man since his creation.
. . . Whenever skeletons are found, they are recognized as either
human or animal, never intermediate. Some skeletons when first
discovered were claimed to be intermediate, but in time they were
seen to be true men."[25]
A. H. Clark states precisely: "There is a sharp, clean-cut, and
very marked difference between man and the apes. Every bone
in the body of a man is at once distinguishable from the corresponding bone in the body of the apes. . . . Man is not an ape, and in
spite of the similarity between them there is not the slightest evidence that man is descended from an ape."[26]

25. *Look Again Before You Doubt* (The American Scientific Affiliation), p. 6.
26. *The New Evolution-Zoogenesis* (Baltimore: Williams and Wilkins, 1930)
p. 224.

11

Genetics

Historical Development

During the dark Middle Ages when superstition abounded, even the means of reproduction were not understood. On walking through the dewy grasses in the morning and seeing the frogs jump on every side, many surmised that frogs arose spontaneously from the dew. Upon finding nests of mice in the drawers and closets, in piles of old rags, many concluded that the mice somehow came into being from the rags. This theory was gradually dispelled when men rediscovered that the Genesis account, written centuries before, was accurate when it said: ". . . God made the beast of the earth *after his kind*. . . ." (1:25). Frogs come from frogs and mice from mice, passing their patterns of traits from generation to generation.

Jean Baptiste Lamarck

Despite the clear evidence in support of the Genesis record, man from time immemorial has attempted to explain his origin other than by creation at the hand of God, because divine creation makes man responsible to God's moral precepts.

A French scientist, Jean Baptiste Lamarck (1744-1829), proposed a theory of evolution some years before Charles Darwin. He believed that if an animal changed its habits or functions, its body structure would be altered. He reasoned, for example, that the giraffe's neck had become long just by stretching upward to feed on tree foliage, each generation inheriting a slightly longer neck. August Weissman (1834-1914), a German biologist working in Vienna, amputated the tails of several generations of rats without obtaining a tailless rat and claimed to have refuted Lamarck's theory. Since this was not comparable to a change in function, it was mediocre evidence against the theory, but the experiment has been widely hailed as a decisive refutation. Weissman's explanation of the continuity of the germ plasm was significant, but Lamarck's theory falls flat before more impressive evidence, namely the governing of inheritance in both plants and animals by chromosomes, about which Lamarck's generation knew little if anything. This will be discussed in more detail later.

Charles Darwin

The name of Charles R. Darwin (1809-1882), an English naturalist, has been associated with the theory of evolution more than any other. While on a voyage on the British ship "Beagle," Darwin noticed the similarity of many related species of finches in the Galapagos Islands and formulated a theory somewhat different from Lamarck's, whose theory Darwin frequently derided. He based his argument on natural selection and "survival of the fittest." Thus, the giraffe developed its long neck because of successive waves of drought in its African habitat, killing the grasses and forcing the beast to reach higher and higher into the trees to obtain foliage. The longer-necked giraffes were thus selected by nature as the fittest to survive. This ignores the many short-necked species that survived in the same habitat and, more important, the effects of climate on arid regions — the trees and not the grasses are the first to die out. The grasses may turn brown, but they will hang on to life while the trees defoliate and die down to and including the roots. One can drive hundreds of miles through treeless grasslands in our western prairies and plateaus and witness mute testimony to this truth. The same is true of the desert areas in Africa.

We see, then, some of the outstanding weaknesses of Darwin's theory: (1) It does not stand the test of logic. For example, if a small furry animal began to develop wings in the front paws, it would pass through gradual stages over millions of years when these front extremities would be neither paws nor wings but excess baggage. It would therefore become extinct quickly, being eliminated through natural selection by those with more efficient limbs, and could never attain the development of the wings of the bat as Darwinians assume. (2) The fossil record does not support it. We do not find in fossil state the intermediate forms that would be necessary for gradual evolutionary change. Instead, we find in the deepest fossil-bearing rocks plant and animal remains which are virtually indistinguishable from modern forms, along with other species (not intermediate) which have become extinct.

Considering these weaknesses, one may well ask why the name of Darwin is almost revered among scientists. For many years, for example, the botany department at Michigan State University held an annual "Darwin Dinner," on the birthday of the great demigod. At one university well known to the author, the Science School Honorary Society, comparable to Phi Beta Kappa and similarly named with three Greek letters, made delta the first letter in Darwin's honor. Yet for all this, he was a highly introvertive character. Following his voyage on the "Beagle," he felt himself to be suffering from a degenerative heart disease and retired to his study, shutting himself off from society, except for daily walks and regular horseback riding, for the last fifty years of his life. Dr. A. W. Woodruff, Wellcome Professor at the London School of Hygiene and Tropical Medicine, and a Darwinian, believes that Darwin suffered from a "chronic depressive, obsessional state" which was common in his family.[1]

Darwin's eminence in the eyes of many scientists is not because his theories are supported by a mass of convincing facts; his theories have been greatly modified even by his supporters. Nor can his eminence be attributed to an attractive personality or character; he was a social misfit. He is honored because his theories paved the way for the ultimate rejection of the Word of God as authoritative over the life and thought of unregenerate society, and gave man a false sense of freedom from any obligation to His commandments, which the unregenerate mistakenly considered a form of servitude.

Aldous Huxley, in his article "Confession of a Professed Atheist," commented on this with his usual frankness: "I had motives for not wanting the world to have meaning. . . . The liberation we desired was simultaneously liberation from a certain political and economic system and liberation from a certain system of morality.

---

1. *Medical World News* (November 3, 1967), p. 98.

We objected to the morality because it interfered with our sexual freedom."[2] *Darwin was to them the great liberator,* bursting asunder the shackles of the so-called "blind traditionalism of orthodox Christianity." This will be discussed further in chapter 13.

Hugo DeVries

Hugo DeVries (1848-1935), a Dutch botanist, based another theory of evolution on genetics. He reasoned that evolutionary change comes through "mutations," sudden changes in the genes resulting in a different form of plant or animal. He believed he had observed this in his garden, experimenting with *Oenothera sp.* (evening primrose). A new species, he claimed, came into existence by steps or jumps. It gained a moment of popularity, but was soon discredited. The new "species" were merely different varieties within the same species. Further, the view that the changes one can observe are due simply to rearrangement of the germ plasm already there rather than to the production of new germ plasm has gained wide acceptance. These changes appear somewhat periodically through the years and in much the same manner. For these reasons, DeVries' mutation theory is no longer highly regarded.

Some scientists felt that large, sudden changes, as postulated by DeVries, could be expected if the number of chromosomes was suddenly doubled or tripled. In the University of Michigan graduate school, the writer coauthored a research paper which reported two chromosome races of *Diospyrus virginianum* (persimmon). Although one race has ninety chromosomes and the other sixty (fig. 29), it is virtually impossible to distinguish the two except by studying the chromosomes under a microscope.[3] The seeds of

2. Aldous Huxley, *Report* (June, 1966), p. 19.
3. J. T. Baldwin and Richard Culp, "Polyploidy in Diospyrus virginiana L.," *American Journal of Botony,* 28 (December, 1941), pp. 942-944.

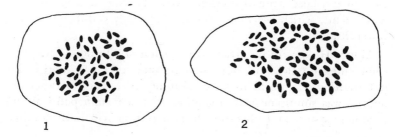

1   2

Fig. 29. Polyploidy in persimmon

those with ninety chromosomes were usually slightly larger, but they were obviously the same species and are always regarded as such. The same relationship of chromosome races has been found within many other species. This, again, offers the evolutionist no real help.

Despite Darwin's interesting observations while aboard the "Beagle," his theories and those of Lamarck and DeVries were founded more on philosophy and speculation than on evidence. Darwin's presumptions and assumptions are in evidence all through his writings. An example was his theory that tiny particles, which he called "gemmules," were constantly migrating to the reproductive organs from other parts of the body. This theory rested on his view that changes in the environment could cause changes in the offspring, not on any scientific evidence. It remained for later investigations to bring the study of inheritance into the realm of true scientific endeavor. By far the most important of these investigations were conducted by Gregor Mendel, whose conclusions were based on precise scientific experimentation which could not be refuted.

Gregor Mendel

Mendel (1822-1884), an Austrian monk, discovered the fundamental laws of inheritance (fig. 30) by crossbreeding peas in the monastery garden. These laws were:

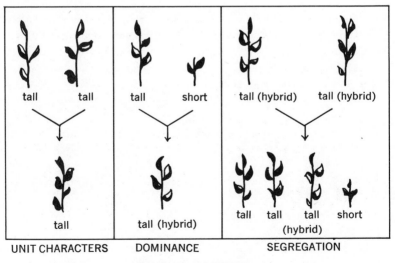

UNIT CHARACTERS   DOMINANCE   SEGREGATION

Fig. 30. Laws of inheritance

The law of unit characters. Mendel first self-pollinated his pea blossoms to obtain a pure strain. When these pea seeds were planted, he found that *tall peas always produced tall offspring.* Short peas always produced short ones. Pure stock (for any one trait) breeds true, although each character is inherited independently of other characters. For example, a pea could be pure for tallness, but hybrid for flower color. He found that, in addition to tallness and flower color, traits such as yellow or green seeds were inherited in the same way. This law favors not change but stability of the species, for like begets like.

The law of dominance. When pure tall peas were crossed with pure short peas, the resulting seed produced *all* tall peas. Mendel called this the F_1 generation. Thus tallness dominated shortness. Also, red flowers dominated white flowers; and yellow seeds, green seeds. Tallness, red flowers, and yellow seeds he called *dominant;* shortness, white flowers, and green seeds, *recessive.* Dominance is sometimes incomplete, as in the pink four-o'clock stemming from red and white blossoming parents.

The law of segregation. When the flowers of the resulting tall peas of the F_1 generation were crossed, instead of all tall plants, which one might have expected, one-fourth of the plants resulting from this second cross (called the F_2 generation) were short. Thus, shortness had not blended into tallness nor had tallness obliterated the inherited character of shortness; it had merely masked it over. Three-fourths of the F_2 generation were tall; one-fourth were short. On further self-pollination of the tall ones, he found that some were pure and some were hybrids; the ratio was one pure tall, two hybrid tall, and one pure short. If 1000 crosses were made, the proportion would always be 1:2:1. Since the recessive character is not bred out, but continues to reappear in successive generations, this again argues for the unchangeable or stable character of inherited traits.

Although Mendel summarized his research in a paper read before the Natural History Society of Brunn, Austria, in 1866, little attention was paid to it, and it sank into oblivion until 1900 when his principles were rediscovered independently by DeVries and Correns.

At first, evolutionists hailed Mendel's findings as additional support for evolution, but the more they studied his experiments and those of his successors, the less encouragement they received. A bombshell had fallen into their midst. Professor William Bateson stated that Darwin would never have written the *Origin of Species* if he had known of Mendel's work.[4]

Other laws of inheritance, and the way in which they affect the species, are:

The continuity or permanence of the germ plasm. Acquired characteristics are not inherited, for inheritance comes from the germ plasm (in reproductive cells) that is passed on from generation to generation unchanged for species characteristics.

Variability. A great variability is possible within a species, but these variations are self-limited because:

a. For every "mutation" in the direction of tallness there will be a "mutation" for shortness according to the laws of chance, and over the years they will cancel off each other.

b. Organisms that are far from the norm tend to be less well adapted to their environment and hence less equipped to survive.

c. Cytological (microscopic) studies show that, when "mutations" arise by a segment being lost from or added to a chromosome, some minor change will show itself in the resulting organism, and this change ordinarily will not improve but hinder chances for survival.

Professor Hermann J. Muller, who received the Nobel Prize for his production of mutations by X-rays, pointed out: ". . . in more than 99 percent of cases the mutation of a gene produces some kind of harmful effect. . . . This disturbance is sometimes enough to kill with certainty any individual who has inherited a mutant gene of the same kind from both his parents. Such a gene is called lethal. More often the effect is not fully lethal but only somewhat detrimental, giving rise to some risk of premature death or failure to reproduce."[5]

d. Many variations do not indicate any structural differences. For example, the common chicory which normally is blue also has white and purple forms. Disease resistance in plants and animals also exemplifies this principle.

Stability of the Species

The experimental laboratory has brought forth some interesting evidence of the permanence of a species. After several decades of breeding experiments with *Drosophila* (fruit flies), the scientists have produced white-eyed, bar-eyed, short-winged, dwarfed, and

---

4. Nelson, *After Its Kind,* p. 119.
5. H. J. Muller, "Radiation and Human Mutation," *Scientific American* (November, 1955), p. 58.

hairless flies, but have not succeeded in developing a new species. Nor has any other species ever been observed changing into another.

In 1952 some Japanese workmen found an ancient canoe buried under eighteen feet of earth in a peat bog near Tokyo. The workmen referred the canoe to archaeologists, who estimated it to be two thousand years old and discovered in it three oriental lotus seeds. These were given to Dr. Ichirohga, Japan's lotus expert, and he planted them. Only one sprouted, but it was planted in an iron cauldron and its growth watched and recorded carefully. Its development was exactly like the oriental lotus in Japan today. Finally, after a four-day watch the bud opened into a beautiful pink blossom and remained open for four days. (See fig. 31.) "It just goes to show you," observed the scientist, "that plants do not undergo evolutionary change in 2,000 years; even the size and the

Fig. 31. Dr. Ichirohga of Japan looks closely at the lotus flower which sprouted from a seed archaeologists estimated to be two thousand years old. The Japanese scientist could find no trace of evolution in the lotus during the last two millennia. (Courtesy of United Press International.)

color is the same."[6] Absolutely no change in two thousand years!

In 1954 a mining engineer working in the Yukon Territory discovered a store of arctic lupine seeds carefully buried by rodents. The seeds, estimated to be ten thousand years old, were entrusted to Canadian botanists who succeeded in germinating six of them. They "produced plants indistinguishable from ordinary arctic lupines."[7]

Furthermore, as we have seen, we can reach still further back in the fossil record and find species that are unchanged. Observe this arresting admission: "California's Calico Mountains have yielded fossilized aquatic insects 25 million years old — the oldest ever found. Discovered by a U. S. Geological Survey team, the specimens included mites, dragonfly nymphs, fairy shrimps. Almost all were perfectly preserved and showed only minute differences from their modern counterparts."[8] Representing arachnids, insects, and crustaceans, they are the oldest ever found and are virtually indistinguishable from the same modern types today!

Chromosomes

With the discovery of the microscope, a whole new world of living creatures, previously unknown, was discovered. Darting protozoa, glittering minute algae, whirling rotifers, and eventually bacteria were found to captivate the pioneer microscope builders like Leeuwenhoek in Holland. Shortly afterward the cellular structure of larger plants and animals became known, and, as higher magnifications and staining techniques were developed, the study of the internal structure of an individual cell became possible. The cell wall and cell membrane, the nucleus, vacuoles and other structures were distinguished and named. Finally, the internal structure of the nucleus (which is the denser center that governs the cell activities) could be studied. It was found that the nucleus was of supreme importance in cell division and reproduction, and that it went through the phases diagrammed in figure 32.

In stage four the chromosomes cross over one another. This phase is called *chiasmata* (literally, "crosses"). In this state the two partners actually exchange parts, resulting in new combinations of genes (the units of inheritance), as seen in figure 33.

---

6. *Time* (August 11, 1952), pp. 58-60. Reprinted by permission.

7. *Organic Gardening and Farming* (September, 1971) p. 23. Refers to an article in *Crops and Soils* (June-July, 1971).

8. *Time* (August 23, 1954), p. 54. Reprinted by permission.

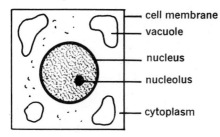

cell membrane
vacuole
nucleus
nucleolus
cytoplasm

1. Resting stage.

2. Chromatin threads appear.

3. Threads thicken and shorten to form chromosomes.

4. Threads pair off, split, and "cross over" (in reproductive cells).

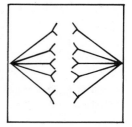

5. Chromosomes form two rows and migrate to opposite ends of the cell.

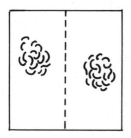

6. Chromosomes regroup to form two nuclei. A new membrane divides the two daughter cells.

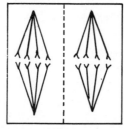

7. In reproductive cells, each daughter cell divides again in the "reduction division."

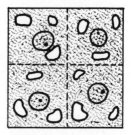

8. Return to the resting stage.

Fig. 32. Stages of cell division and meiosis

One can see immediately how this phase profoundly affects the inherited traits of the offspring. It would seem no mere coincidence that in this stage, when the final inheritance pattern is affected so greatly, the chromosomes are forming crosses all over the cell. As the potential of physical traits is greatly influenced at the stage

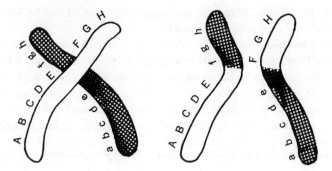

Fig. 33. "Crossing over" of chromosomes

characterized by a cross, so the immense possibilities of the spiritual man are manifest as one comes to the cross of Jesus Christ for forgiveness of sin and for the power of the Spirit of God in his heart and life.

Heredity and Environment

We can easily see how one could believe that heredity is the single most important factor in determining overall characteristics, as some assert, for it determines the color of our eyes, hair, and skin, whether we shall be tall or short, active or lethargic, and (to some degree) thin or obese. It even determines the length and shape of the nose. We have already seen the importance of heredity in domesticated animals.

On the other hand, many feel that environment is a more important factor. We can take a "scrub cow" with limited inherited possibilities and discover that, with the best possible feed and care, it will do better than a pedigreed cow kept on a diet deficient in vitamins, proteins, and minerals, and given inadequate care. We have often heard of puny boys who have built strong bodies by careful exercise, some becoming champion distance runners. Even in the religious realm this influence is well known. A man born in a Catholic home in a Catholic country is likely to be Catholic; one born in a Lutheran home in a Lutheran country probably will be Lutheran.

Both schools of thought overlook some very important factors. Man is no mere automaton, a blend of heredity and environment, as is the beast of the field. God has given each man a *free will* with which to choose from the physical and mental assets that his heredity and environment provide.

The power of choice also opens up a fourth factor. When one chooses God's way of salvation through faith in the blood of Christ, he is baptized by the Spirit of God (I Cor. 12:13) and walks in the power of the Spirit. Heredity and environment may explain man's characteristics to a large measure in his life and labors without Christ and the Holy Spirit. However, when he is born again by the Spirit of God, he partakes of the divine nature (II Peter 1:4) and is given by the Spirit various spiritual gifts (like the gift of teaching), to exercise in the kingdom of God with a power that is quite unknown to the unbeliever. For this reason we must constantly look beyond a man's family background, his educational qualifications, and his secular experiences to his spiritual stature when deciding whether he is qualified for any particular place of service in the kingdom of God.

Domesticated Plants and Animals

While I was working for the U. S. Department of Agriculture at the University of Nebraska, my superior was a well-known horticulturist who had developed commercial varieties of vegetables. He had developed a certified seed industry of a vegetable in that state. He was not known for humility. Although reared in a Protestant church in eastern Pennsylvania, he had become more and more agnostic in college. He migrated to a more liberal church and finally to the Unitarian church, which denies the inspiration of the Scriptures, the deity of Christ, and the personality of the Holy Spirit. He tried to appear calm when I witnessed to him of my Christian conversion, but it appeared to require no little self-control. I never broached the subject of evolution to him, feeling that sometime he would raise the issue.

He did on a sunny autumn day while we were driving through Nebraska's fascinating Sand Hills toward the experimental farm in the western part of the state. With an arrogant chuckle, he began as a cat teases with a mouse that has surely met its doom.

"We can see," he said, "evolution all around us. Our blooded dairy herds are now producing many times the gallons of milk per cow that they did some years ago. Our chickens can produce several times the number of eggs in comparison to their ancestors of but a few decades back. Our waving fields of grain testify to the increase in yield and quality that has been produced through change at the hand of man. The vegetables you have been working with show marked improvement in yield and quality. And then there is the fossil record. All of these things are evidence of evolution!" I waited until he finished. I did not then have a doctor's degree, but I had taken most of the college courses that taught evolution, making it a subject of special study. I often spent hours studying the other side of the question when a professor was "pouring on" the evolution in class. Beyond the general course in genetics, I had taken two advanced courses and had written a graduate research paper on cytogenetics. I had worked at two other agricultural experiment stations and at the University of Michigan's Botanical Gardens. Even more important, I had prayed frequently that the Lord would guide me to the truth and help me stand for it.

After he finished, I began rather slowly. I reviewed the matter of mutation: according to the laws of chance (a favorite phrase of the geneticist), for every deviation in one direction there is a compensating deviation in the opposite direction, so that these cancel off and the species remains unchanged. The fossil record agrees; many fossils are identical to modern forms, and the remainder have simply become extinct without any modern species evolving from them. [This is somewhat oversimplified, but it is further explained in another chapter].

I then turned to the subject of domesticated plants and animals. "As I recall my study of genetics, the evolutionist almost always argues from the standpoint of *natural selection* in order to produce any change in yield or quality. [At that time this was true.] But, in order to produce any new varieties (they are not new species), it is absolutely essential to *prevent* natural selection. That is why we must carefully maintain our bloodlines of registered cattle and control the selection of sire and dam, for if we allow free or random breeding (as in natural selection), they will soon take on characteristics of "scrub cows" [which he well knew]. If we do not maintain our bloodlines in poultry we will soon have the wild type of low-producing hens. For the same reason we must keep those little paper bags on our tomato and potato plants to produce controlled crosses. We must *prevent natural selection* or we shall soon have the small, wild-type tomato and potato. Further, the changes made by artificial breeding do not make the variety hardier but less fit to survive. When we want disease resistance in our tomato plants, we must go back to the wild South American tomato to breed its resistance into our large-fruiting tomatoes. Natural selection maintains the species." I rested my case with all the enthusiasm and conviction of an electric sweeper salesman.

As we rolled on, only the purr of the pickup motor broke the silence. The veteran agnostic professor was obviously groping for words. Finally he said, "Well, you may be a voice in the wilderness; you seem to enjoy it!" He had seen his case for evolution collapse — and in his own field of study! This indicated not that I was any brighter than he, but that he had blindly accepted the evolutionary indoctrination which he had received in college and could no longer detect contrary evidence even in his own field. It showed that, in any fair discussion, God's revelation will measure up to the best scientific evidence. The Christian is on the side of the evidence!

The professor's comment turned out to be less generous than it appeared. When I mentioned that the science of archaeology, which is more refined and accurate than biology, is never at variance with the Word of God, he claimed he was "not interested in such ancient subjects." But when he felt he might score a point from the fossil record, he betrayed a deep interest in ancient subjects.

The fact that domesticated animals still retain many masked primitive traits that will come to the surface through natural or random selection was demonstrated dramatically by the breeding experiments carried out by the Munich Zoo director, Hans Heck. He had become interested in the prehistoric paintings of an aurochs, an extinct cow, on the walls of caves in the Pyrenees Mountains. The last recorded specimen of aurochs was killed in Poland in 1629. The aurochs was the ancestor of our modern breeds of cattle, so Heck carefully selected the more primitive traits in each generation of cattle for a number of generations and, with patience and skill, produced a strain that is remarkably parallel to its extinct progenitor. Dr. William Mann, then director of the National Zoo in Washington, D.C., viewed these modern aurochs on a tour of European zoos. He explained, "Hans finally got what he wanted — a 20th century aurochs. He showed me half a dozen cows that are 'dead ringers' for the extinct species — massive sluggish beasts, with a strange white stripe down the back. You'd take them for prehistoric animals at a glance"[9] (fig. 34). Heck also re-created the tarpan, the ancient wild horse which is also found in paintings in the Pyrenees caverns. The tarpan, apparently relished as food by

---

9. "European Zoos," *Life* (December 6, 1948).

Fig. 34. The aurochs had been extinct for over 300 years when Hans Heck, director of the Munich Zoo, bred one from modern cattle. He carefully selected the more primitive traits from each generation, proving that such traits exist and that the modern cow did not evolve but was artificially bred. (Courtesy of United Press International.)

the artisans, were fierce, hardy, small in stature, and small-boned, with gray fur, striped legs, short manes, broad skulls, and mooselike noses. He crossbred Przewalsky's horse, the last truly wild horse, found by Przewalsky (a Russian explorer) in the 1880s, with more primitive type mares from among modern horses found in Iceland and Gotland. Again, by selecting the primitive types from each generation, he succeeded in producing a horse with all the characteristics of the ancient tarpan, which had become extinct about 1877 (fig. 35).

One might expect these primitive strains to be better equipped to survive hardships, and this is the case; they have unusual resistance to disease. "The day may come," said Dr. Heck, "when

Fig. 35. The tarpan bred by Hans Heck (top) is remarkably similar to its ancient, extinct counterpart (bottom). This experiment, like the one with the aurochs (see fig. 34), demonstrates that modern horses did not evolve; they were bred. (Courtesy of Mrs. Hans Heck and Munich Zoo.)

our highly bred, high strung modern breeds will need a shot of
their wild ancestors' blood to revitalize them."[10]

---

10. "Looking Backward," *Time* (December 1, 1942, p. 42).

12

Evolutionists' Weaknesses

This section contains many of the writer's personal experiences, on the belief that some benefit should accrue from information gathered firsthand.

Disunity

Inasmuch as the basis of evolution is largely philosophical, one should expect wide variations in the views of evolutionists. This is precisely the case. In our course of advanced genetics at the University of Michigan, we learned of the hot-pitched battle concerning chromosomal structure between Darlington and Bell, both outstanding geneticists. The argument became bitter and heated; both were guilty of emotional excess, although Darlington seemed to be the more antagonistic and provoking of the two. The fact that their two theories were so far apart makes one suspect that neither man was sure of his ground.

John C. Willis proposed the "age and area" theory: if one selects ten species from each of two or more genera of plants and animals, the land area that the ten species cover is in proportion to the number of centuries the genus has existed. For example, if total surface area of ten species of the cabbage group exceeds that of the tomato group, the cabbage group evolved first. But this theory was considered little more than a joke by plant anatomists and paleontologists. Dr. C. A. Arnold, for example, pointed to the bracken fern, which has been found only in higher rock strata, but which has one of the greatest distributions of any living plant!

Another controversy in my student days was caused by Goldschmidt's book on evolution. In my notes from "Advanced Genetics" is this statement about Goldschmidt's text: "His concept is not that of traditional natural selection, and this provoked antagonism and heated opposition by his fellow scientists."

The great majority of science students in college gain the impression that the evolution of the horse, for example, is well-established, when in fact it is a matter of debate. A brief article entitled, "Little Eohippus No Direct Ancestor of the Horse," reads:

> The ancestral family tree of the horse is not what scientists have thought it to be.
> Professor T. S. Westall, Durham University geologist, told the British Association of the Advancement of Science at Edinburgh, that the early classical evolutionary tree of the horse, beginning in the small dog-sized Eohippus and tracing directly to Equus, was all wrong.
> The direct line of descendents of Eohippus led to a horselike animal, Hypohippus, which became extinct and thus ended the line.[1]

Fluctuation

When I was a boy, the nebular hypothesis for the origin of the earth — that it came from the sun — was very popular. Later, the planar theory came to the forefront. Both have many difficulties. "Not to know history is to be always a child." The earth had supposedly come from the sun and cooled off, so it was common to believe that it was still cooling off. Sunday newspaper supplements depicted man one day building elaborate tunnels and underground storehouses in order to survive extremes in temperature similar to those now found on the moon's surface. We need hardly say that these assertions disagree with facts recorded by scientists. If there is any change in long-range temperatures, it is upward rather than downward. Eskimos are reportedly moving farther north to hunt seals, and the fish on which the seals feed are moving north to find sufficiently cool water. Also, the glaciers in the United States and Canada are gradually diminishing in size. These changes come in cycles.

---

1. *Science Newsletter* (August 25, 1951), p. 18. Reprinted with permission.

While theories fluctuate as markedly as fashions in attire, scientists too often support the latest theory dogmatically. Dr. Harold C. Urey of the University of Chicago, recipient of the Nobel Prize in chemistry in 1934 for his discovery of heavy hydrogen (deuterium), had the courage to speak to this point when he addressed the annual physics colloquium at the University of Iowa in June, 1950. The internationally known authority on chemistry and the structure of the atom declared, "All suggestions as to the origin of the earth are partly right and partly wrong." The *Iowa City Press-Citizen* reported that he "discounted the notion that any theory is complete. He said that a year ago he had been asked to teach a course on the subject, and the more he learned the less he felt he knew."[2]

Closed-mindedness

When studying in graduate school at the University of Michigan, I testified of the evidence against evolution to other graduate students in the same department. Most were reasonable and tolerant, but there was one exception, an apostate from Judaism who displayed proudly a large portrait of Einstein over his desk. Einstein was his hero, for he also had descended from Judaism into the darkness of agnosticism, if not atheism. The arrogant student may even have fancied a close similarity between Einstein's keen mind and his own. At any rate, I enjoyed presenting to him the evidence against the concept of fossil ape-men. When I revealed the fact that the "reconstructions" of these fictitious monsters were based on a few pieces of bones (that in some cases did not even belong together), he was forced to retreat from the accuracy of the evidence to the "authority" of the reconstructors. "If you knew as much as they know," he steamed, "you would not be so confident of your position." Then I explained how little you could depend on their "authority"; Smith-Woodward decided that the skull of Piltdown man was subhuman with a capacity of 1050cc, whereas Sir Arthur Keith had considered it clearly human with a capacity of 1500cc. Further, the jawbone had been clearly identified as a chimpanzee's by anthropologists of the highest repute on both sides of the Atlantic. I have often wondered if he remembered this conversation when, some years later, the Piltdown man was publicly exposed as a hoax. He certainly had been standing on scanty, untrustworthy information.

---

2. June 16, 1950, p. 2.

Professor E. A. Hooton, long a foe of speculation, writes forcibly:

> Some anatomists model reconstructions of fossil skulls by build-
> ing up the soft parts of the head and face upon a skull case, and
> thus produce a bust purporting to represent the appearance of
> the man in life. When, however, we recall the fragmentary condi-
> tion of most of the skulls, the faces usually being missing, we can
> readily see that even the reconstruction of the facial skeleton
> leaves room for a good deal of doubt as to details. The various
> reconstructions of the skull of Piltdown Man by Smith-Wood-
> ward, Keith, and other experts, differ widely one from another.
> To attempt to restore the soft parts is an even more hazardous
> undertaking. The lips, the eyes, the ears, and the nasal tip, leave
> no clue on the underlying bony parts. You can with equal facility
> model on a Neanderthal skull the features of a chimpanzee or
> the lineaments of a philosopher. These alleged restorations of
> ancient types of man have very little, if any, scientific value, and
> are likely only to mislead the public. To model a bust of
> **Pithecanthropus erectus** from the skull cap and the two or
> three teeth is a palpable absurdity. We do not know anything
> of the minutiae of the appearance of the Pithecanthropus, Heidel-
> berg, Piltdown, or Neanderthal types. We have no knowledge of
> their hair form, hair distribution, pigmentation, and the detail
> of such features as I have mentioned. So put not your trust in
> reconstructions.[3]

Some time ago Professor W. B. Scott wrote: "My experience with
graduate students of biology has shown me that usually their training has so completely taken for granted the truth of the evolutionary doctrine, that they have but a vague conception of the testimony by which that doctrine is supported."[4] My observation has
been the same; human nature has not changed.

Fallibility

Occasionally, blunders even worse than unwarranted reconstructions are made. Dr. C. A. Arnold told us in one of his paleobotany
lectures about a fossil which was proudly displayed by one of America's foremost museums of natural history. Billed as the most primitive corn yet discovered, it was officially classified and given the
scientific name of *Zea antiqua*.

Unfortunately for the display, a curious young scientist who
came to work at the museum had the audacity to gently scratch the
surface with a knife and examine it with a hand lens, only to dis-

---

3. *Up from the Ape* (New York: Macmillan, 1931), p. 332.
4. *The Theory of Evolution* (New York: Macmillan, 1917), p. 10.

cover that the widely heralded "fossil" was a specimen of Peruvian pottery, an Indian artifact!

LeGros Clark, an evolutionist, gives an interesting example of a surprisingly gross error caused by scanty measurements: "An example of this difficulty is provided by the famous case of *Hesperopithecus*. This generic name was given to a fossil tooth found in Nebraska in 1922, on the assumption that it represented an extinct type of anthropoid ape . . . the tooth proved later to be that of a fossil peccary [a pig-like mammal]. . . . There can be few paleontologists who have not erred in this way at some time or another!"[5]

We have mentioned the bones of Piltdown man, purposely treated for fraudulent purposes, but accepted as authentic by the vast majority of scientists for a number of years.

Credulity

Whitcomb and Morris call attention to the fact that "the so-called historical geology . . . has not changed or developed in any essential particular for over a hundred years, since the days when its basic philosophical structure was first worked out by such non-geologists as Charles Lyell (a lawyer), William Smith (a surveyor), James Hutton (an agriculturist), John Playfair (a mathematician), Georges Cuvier (a comparative anatomist and the only creationist in the group), Charles Darwin (an apostate divinity student turned naturalist), and various theologians (Buckland, Fleming, Pye Smith, and Sedgewick)."[6]

Evolution has become so popular, however, that geologists, biologists, and anthropologists with extensive training at the graduate level now accept it without question, as we have already noted, and for the most part without knowing its crude origins and history. It scarcely need be said that those who sit at their feet and the vast numbers who never attend college are likewise uninformed but thoroughly persuaded, trusting the word of the "great men of science." Occasionally some from their ranks become so confident of the position of organic evolution that they became self-appointed authorities and critics of special creation.

An example is Martin Gardner, author of the paperback, *Fads and Fallacies*. He is not a trained scientist and admits that "most

5. *The Fossil Evidence for Human Evolution*, pp. 26f.
6. *The Genesis Flood*, p. xxvii.

of my research was done in the New York Public Library,"[7] but he assails with vigor and occasional vitriolic impatience the scientific theories with which he disagrees. Some, such as the "hollow earth theory," have been accepted primarily by the gullible, but others, such as organic gardening, have been established by thorough and repeated research. He also attacks special creation, using indiscriminate broadside attacks and guilt by association that hardly belong in the realm of science. He describes the book, *The Dogma of Evolution,* written in 1925 by Dr. Louis T. More, professor of physics at the University of Cincinnati, as "an infuriating book" that uses "all the old and outworn arguments."[8] Maybe the author was infuriated because he could not refute the arguments, something he does not attempt to do. The "old and outworn arguments" were drawn from solid biological facts and frustrate the critic. He ridicules the argument of fossil formation by flood waters, but fails to give one scientific argument against it.[9]

My roommate at the University of Michigan, a fundamentalist who was nearing his doctorate degree, asked me confidentially whether I felt a Christian could be an evolutionist. I sensed he was faltering a little before the constant indoctrination we received in one class after another. My reply was that perhaps one could philosophically, but that the scientific evidence would not support it. I said nothing at this time about the Bible. I gave him some sound Christian booklets and made him a matter of prayer. Later he confided that he had asked his professor about it, which of course I would never recommend to a student. His professor was the outstanding attraction on the faculty, a recognized authority in both cytology and the study of algae. At that time students came from Java, India, and China to study under him. His answer was most surprising: "I do not accept the Bible account, but I can tell you one thing, *there is no theory of evolution that you can't poke holes in.*" Unfortunately such statements never find their way into the "scientific" journals. He was a living demonstration of the fact that the evolutionist is not forced to his view, as is often claimed, by overwhelming evidence.

Inhibition of Dissent

Some outstanding scientists have repudiated evolution. The Crea-

7. (New York: Dove Publications), p. viii.
8. Ibid., p. 37.
9. Ibid., chap. 11.

tion Research Society is a strong organization of scientists who believe in special creation and publish a stimulating quarterly journal. They are men with advanced training in every major branch of science. In recent years, they have produced many new books and booklets. They are giving themselves to the propagation and defense of the historic Christian view of creation, as upheld by the Scriptures and vindicated by modern scientific evidence. We shall hear more of them later.

Many others, some of whom are not even Christians, object to some or all of the evolutionary theories, but they see no point in making this public because they would only be discredited by the thorough-going, committed evolutionists. In addition, their views would not be published in scientific journals because they are controlled by evolutionists. Scholastically it is often hazardous for a Christian to publically repudiate evolution, but a few have had the courage to do it.

I observed this at close hand on several occasions. For example, the professor of physiology at Purdue University had been introducing considerable evolutionary teaching in his courses, but our weekly discussion period was led by another teacher. One day he asked the class how many still did not, after the senior professor's indoctrination, believe in evolution. I held up my hand and so did a girl. With an air of respect, he asked for my reasons. In somewhat stumbling fashion, I related my misgivings about the countless "missing links" in the evolutionary scale and the apparent permanence of many species found in fossil form. Today I would consider that explanation as somewhat crude, but it represented my sincere convictions. When the girl was asked for her reasons, she replied that she felt the same way. And then, in the moment which followed, one which I shall never forget, the instructor said without apology, "And I guess I would agree with him." Later I heard that he was a Christian. How important it is that we take our stand on this issue! This might have been the turning point in the life of some student in the class who was later able to emerge from the labyrinth of unbelief and find Christ as his Savior.

Again, in a course in advanced genetics, I was assigned a special report. With a sense of satisfaction I quoted directly from the scientific literature (while the professor shifted uneasily in his chair) to show that the southern wild irises had undergone no apparent evolutionary change.

About this time a zoologist in the class, who sensed the professor's obvious dogmatism, asked a disturbing question. "Isn't it true that many investigators tend to be overenthusiastic in explaining things in terms of evolutionary significance?" The professor countered, "Yes, but it is only natural that one should try to explain things." It was apparent that the professor's bias prevented his considering any explanation that disagreed with the theory of evolution. This is not a scientific approach.

I recall a dull class in educational biology, during which the instructor, wearing his usual frozen smile, attempted to impress us with the importance and relevance of "seven cardinal principles of secondary education." They were: (1) health, (2) command of fundamental processes, (3) worthy home membership, (4) vocational education, (5) civic competence, (6) worthy use of leisure time, (7) development of ethical character. He began to wax eloquent and overflow with enthusiasm as he compared these principles to a mighty lens which we should use in selecting our teaching material and bringing into focus the great truths of biology. At the end of the oration he asked for questions from his half-slumbering audience. In the absence of any other questions, I asked which of these seven principles he would use to justify the teaching of evolution, which he had been actively promoting in the classroom. Fortunately for him his smile was frozen, and he somehow managed to maintain it. He smiled, tried to begin, sputtered, and smiled again, but try as he would, he could not then — nor did he ever —answer the question. It was striking evidence that his teaching on evolution violated the very standards which he urged us to uphold. After class one of the students remarked, "At least you broke the monotony today for a change." My grade also fell a full letter!

When I was a teaching assistant at Michigan State University, my conviction grew that I should testify for the truth on this question in my course. I had complete charge of the two-hour plant physiology laboratory, which was usually introduced by thirty to forty minutes of explaining the principles that would be tested and the procedure the students should follow. One day the subject lent itself perfectly to a discussion of evolution, which the professor had been hammering in his lectures.

"I realize," I told the class, "that in your courses of study you have heard frequent arguments in favor of organic evolution. I thought you may be interested in hearing the evidence on the other side of the question." For about thirty minutes I reviewed the evidence from the various fields of study. These students, seasoned by many months of evolutionary dogma, sat in rapt attention; when I finished, you could have heard a pin drop. They were amazed at the amount of evidence which their professors had either not known or artfully concealed.

Philosophical Orientation

A student once came to me in the plant physiology laboratory to ask a question about the course. A visiting instructor from England happened to be in the laboratory at that time. He had no responsibility for the course in plant physiology, but he flagrantly usurped my authority and answered the student before I could reply. The instructor strolled to the blackboard and with characteristic confidence answered with some arguments supporting evolution. After he finished, I smiled and asked if this problem couldn't be explained just as well by special creation.

"Creation!" he snorted, betraying his emotional bias. He quickly recovered, however, and the student soon left, knowing at least that there were two sides to the question.

Afterward, as the instructor and I chatted in a more friendly vein, I reviewed the evidence against evolution from comparative anatomy, embryology, geology, and genetics, much as it has been presented in these chapters. With no one else listening and with no face-saving to pressure him, he became remarkably amenable to reason. He admitted that none of the evidence usually given in support of evolution proved it to be true! Then he gave his own reasons, which were so broadly philosophical that they did not rest on scientific evidence at all. But he still believed in evolution, obviously because it met an emotional need. We shall say more concerning these principles later.

Forty years elapsed between the discovery of Piltdown man and its repudiation. This is a long time for such a monstrous error to be foisted on an unsuspecting laity as scientific evidence for the existence of ape-men. William L. Straus, Jr., Johns Hopkins University anthropologist, explains in the February 26, 1954, issue of *Science* why it took so long to discover the hoax. First, there was no reason to suspect a hoax until fluorine tests were made. (However, he must admit that reputed anthropologists had recognized the jaw as that of a chimpanzee.)

His second reason, however, is more illuminating. By carefully documented quotations, he shows that anthropologists had already decided that the brain developed into a fully human organ before the rest of the body. This laid the groundwork for them to associate the clearly human skull fragments with the ape-like jaw. Straus concludes with this surprisingly honest admission: "It is a demonstration, furthermore, that the . . . nature of the pages of man's history is not always due directly to new fossil discoveries but can also result from *changes in the philosophical climate* of the science. That this phenomenon is peculiar to anthropology, however, is seriously to be doubted." (Emphasis mine.)

This underscores the instability of prevailing philosophies among evolutionists, because the very opposite view is now used to justify Leaky's *Australopithecus* "restoration": the rest of the skull developed manlike features while the brain case remained ape-like.

Needless to say, the unsuspecting layman is entirely unaware of the philosophical basis for the evolutionist's views, believing that his conclusions are based on proven scientific facts.

Anthony Standen, an entomologist, gently tweaked the noses of the evolutionists in his interesting volume, *Science Is a Sacred Cow,* likening their philosophical platform to a house of cards. He shows that the genealogical "trees" Haekel designed to prove evolution have fallen to pieces because of the lack of intermediate forms: "There ought to be a whole series of animals going up the main trunk and out along all the branches . . . there aren't any."[10]

Occasionally in graduate school some of my good colleagues would ask, "Why do some people try to disprove evolution, anyway?"

The "scientific method" has been drilled into the science student from his earliest studies of the subject, but he seems to forget it when considering the theory of evolution. The steps in the scientific method are:

1. Select a definite problem to solve.

2. Collect evidence, often library evidence, to see if the problem is solvable and how.

3. Form a hypothesis, a scientific guess, about what the answer may be.

4. Test the hypothesis by experiment, observation, or measurement, using a control to compare it with.

5. Form a conclusion as to whether the hypothesis was correct.

---

10. (New York: E. P. Dutton), p. 105.

6. Test the hypothesis by experiment to see *if the hypothesis can be disproven.* (Emphasis mine.)

Observe particularly the last step; it is most important. The zealous scientist, anxious to make an impressive case, may slight the last step. This can be fatal to his cause, however, and may eventually bring him to disrepute. One professor at Michigan State University, for example, in his younger years, thought he had found evidence for structures within plant cells that had never been reported. He prepared many slides from his findings and, despite some friendly warnings to check his data carefully, presented a paper at a national convention of scientists. The first reaction was that a monumental discovery in cellular structure had been made, and a brilliant young scientist was on the threshold of fame. His triumph was fleeting, however, for in a few hours an investigator from the University of Wisconsin produced extensive and incontrovertible evidence that the "new structures" were merely artifacts (artificial sediments in the cells from the dyes and fixative used in preparing the slides), and the young scientist went home in disgrace.

When one questions the reasons for trying to disprove evolution, he casts doubt on the scientific method itself. Any scientist worthy of the name should be willing to consider all arguments contrary to his working hypothesis and to try to disprove them.

Avoiding the question, "Is it possible that evolution *as a working principle* is not valid?" is also contrary to inductive reasoning (moving from specific facts to the general conclusion), and the scientific method rests upon inductive reasoning. The scientist avows that he draws his conclusions, or forms his hypotheses, only after gathering many specific facts from experimental studies. Without these *specific* facts the conclusions are, of course, without foundation. However, it is no secret that evolutionists are continually faulting each other's arguments and presenting evidence against them. I have been deeply impressed by the fact that, when all the arguments are in and the smoke has cleared, none of the arguments is still standing, for all ignore important scientific data; yet the evolutionists stubbornly refuse to admit that evolution *as a method* has been disproven. Now in this they are departing from inductive reasoning, for if the *specific arguments are untrue, then the broad conclusions based on them, the hypotheses of evolution, are also untrue.* Logic allows no other conclusion.

How well informed are evolutionists? My first hint came when I was a senior in high school. I questioned a classmate about her beliefs on the subject. I was disappointed when she answered, "I believe just like Charles Darwin believed." When I questioned her further about what Darwin believed, or what she thought he believed, she was unable to fill in any details. The shallowness of her knowledge was arresting.

Joining hands with the evolutionist and becoming liberated from the traditions and "religious superstitions of his grandparents" is popular among students in college (and often even in high school). They may have heard only one side of the question, and their knowledge may be meager, but this does not prevent them from feeling they have "arrived" and now stand amid the throngs of the enlightened intelligentsia. In the words of Dr. A. H. Clark: "Biologists are, of course, confessedly evolutionists, but it is really remarkable how little evidence they advance in support of their theories."[11]

This may be credited to the smug assumption that the hypothesis has been proven and requires no further supporting evidence. Contrary evidence may be overlooked or unconsciously ignored. I recall pointing out to an embryology professor goblet cells in my slide of the vermiform appendix. Our professor, formerly on the embryology research staff at Harvard University, remarked somewhat impatiently, "There are no such cells in the appendix." In front of me was our textbook, open to a diagram which showed typical goblet cells in the appendix. This professor was an excellent lecturer, but he was also the most dogmatic evolutionist on the staff, bringing the subject in at every possible turn. The evolutionist teaching that the appendix is vestigial, and that it therefore had no useful function such as the *mucus-producing* goblet cells would afford, made him oblivious to the cells' presence in the appendix.

Dogmatism

At first the promoters of evolution, being in the minority, cried against the "persecution" of those who taught the theory in public institutions, demanding freedom of speech. Evolution appeals to the natural man, who wishes to be "free" from a moral standard based on the Bible, so its advocates eventually became the majority, filling professorships and chairmanships of science departments and acquiring a virtual monopoly. With this came a smugness and one-sided promotion that does not breathe the freedom of thought

---

11. *The New Evolution,* p. 189.

that they once claimed to seek. Often I have heard professors, assistants, and students say, "We do not argue the theory of evolution; we just accept it." It is no longer open to question and they do not bother to consider the other side of the question, a most formidable one at that.

One of my sons revealed that his biology instructor was teaching evolution. I questioned the principal about this, and he showed me the Blue Book, the guide for secondary schools in Pennsylvania, which required schools to teach "historical anthropology." The terms were obviously designed to mislead both legislators and voters as to its true intent. It was revealing that the principal assumed that historical anthropology required the evolutionary concept; he manifested his personal bias, and that of the Book's authors.

Dogmatism hinders, not helps, true science. I recall vividly a botanical seminar at Michigan State University, led by another of the assistants. While the speaker was making a point, the genetics professor, author of a textbook in his field, became visibly annoyed. "Why," he exclaimed, reddening, "that couldn't possibly be true, because if it were, man could not have descended from the amoeba." He intended that to end all argument. I thought to myself, "What a pair of blinders the theory of evolution has placed on that man!"

This dogmatism can be expressed in many ways. One is the slanted use of terms. All scientists use the term *species,* but they do not always agree on what it means. Some are "splitters," dividing into separate species organisms that other scientists consider to be varieties of the same species, while others are "lumpers," grouping forms in larger groups and making fewer species. To make matters still more confusing, many "split" in one direction and "lump" in another, particularly if it fits well into the evolutionary scheme.

It is popular, since racism has become such an issue, to consider all men of the same species. Even the weather-beaten old agnostic claims, "Yep, the Bible is right; all men have descended from the same ancestor." Whether they are pygmies or giants, blond and blue-eyed or black as coal, whether the nose is broad and flaring or narrow and pinched — yes, sir — they are all the same species!

E. K. V. Pearce, while accusing another anthropologist, C. S. Coon, of racial bias, reveals his own inter-racial bias and demonstrates that anthropologists adjust their theories to fit the current popular emphasis on racial equality: "Anthropologists today are very much against feelings of race superiority, and believe very much in the *Homo sapiens* potential equality of all men."[12] Recalling the prevailing theories in anthropology just before the exposure of Piltdown man, just how much trust we can place in an anthropology that accommodates itself to sociological trends?

I agree that all men are of the same species, but one cannot then call the two forms of meadowlark separate species. The eastern meadowlark is classified as *Sturnella magna,* while the western meadowlark is named *Sturnella neglecta.* This is done to give the impression that different species have arisen from the same ancestor, for, as Roger Tory Peterson comments, the western meadowlark is "nearly identical with the eastern meadowlark, but paler, and yellow of throat edging a trifle farther onto the cheek; best recognized by its song."[13] It is usually impossible to distinguish the two by plumage or even from skins; the song is the only dependable criterion. Arthur C. Bent, author of a monograph on the blackbird group to which the meadowlark belongs, agrees: ". . . there is no visible character by which it [the western meadowlark] can be distinguished from the eastern meadowlark."[14]

The ranges of the eastern and western meadowlark overlap in the central states, and there they often may be found nesting in the same fields. There seems to be some intergrading between the two, which one would not expect of separate species, or even of subspecies (although the degree to which this is done has apparently never been carefully studied). This may account for some modification of the western bird's song. A. D. Dubois observes, ". . . in Minnesota we have both species; but in this locality I do not hear quite the same songs of the westerner that I heard in Montana."[15]

Compare these minute differences to those between the big, blond Swede and the tiny, black Negrito, which we are assured belong to the same species. Many of the variations among the finches on the Galapagos Islands, which misled Darwin to formulate his evolutionary theory, are less significant than those found among the human family, yet are considered sufficient for the development of new species. V. Elving Anderson, for example, comments that they are "all gray brown, short-tailed, with fluffy rump feathers. They

---

12. "Proto-neolithic Adam and Recent Anthropology," *Journal of the American Scientific Affiliation* (December, 1971), pp. 130f.

13. *A Field Guide to the Birds* (Boston: Houghton Mifflin Co., 1947), p. 210.

14. *Life Histories of North American Blackbirds, Orioles, Tanagers, and Allies* (New York: Dover Publications, 1965), p. 63.

15. Ibid., p. 91.

build roofed nests, display territoriality, are monogamous. . . . The size varies from that of a small warbler to that of a very large sparrow."[16] Then he quotes David Lack, who observed them in 1928: "Only the variety of the beaks and the number of their species excite attention — small finch-like beaks, huge finch-like beaks, parrot-like beaks, straight wood-boring beaks, . . . species which look very different and species which look closely similar."[17] Lack indulges in some exaggeration here. If you expect to find among them birds that resemble woodpeckers or parrots, a study of their beaks will be disappointing; that there is considerable variation among them will not be denied. Whether these are significant enough to constitute separate species is the issue. Anderson concedes "the possibility that some of the 'species' are merely striking variants which should be considered sub-species"; there is also the possibility of two or more closely related original species. Only the "warblers" have relatively small, thin beaks, whereas all the other beaks are somewhat stout and finch-like (a few are enormously enlarged), so that two natural groupings would seem plausible.

Moreover, recall the great variation of structures among men: variations in body size; short noses among Dyaks versus long noses among Semitic tribes; small Negroid jaw versus Nordic "lantern jaw" and Eskimo massive "block" jaw; long Negroid head versus round Mongoloid head, to mention only a few. Yet the anthropologist assures us that these differences are insufficient to justify separate species.

We conclude, therefore, that such terms as *species* are frequently bent rather acutely by the evolutionist.

Recently there has been a tendency to "lump" some species of birds together, as reported in the *Thirty-Second Supplement to the American Ornithologists' Union Check List of North American Birds*. The *Audubon* reported some of these changes, such as the blue goose now being classified as a color variant of the snow goose, and the red-shafted flicker and gilded flicker all being lumped together as the common flicker, since they have been found to interbreed in some parts of their ranges. (No report was made there, however, of the current status of the meadowlark).[18]

---

16. "The Distribution of Animals," *Evolution and Christian Thought Today*, pp. 127f. Used by permission.
17. *Darwin's Finches* (Cambridge: Cambridge University Press, 1947), p. 11.
18. Robert Arbib, "Hail, Great-Tailed Grackle! Baltimore Oriole, Farewell!" *Audobon*, 75 (November, 1973), pp. 36-39.

Further, many scientists have serious misgivings about considering two similar organisms separate species if they will not hybridize or if they produce sterile hybrids. There are too many proven exceptions. J. A. Moore, for example, demonstrated that crosses between strains of the same species of frog, *Rana pipiens*, from widely separated areas produced defective offspring, whereas crosses between *Rana pipiens* and *Rana palustris* produced hybrids that were normal and fertile.[19] Wilbur L. Bullock, associate professor of zoology at the University of New Hampshire, mentions other exceptions (like the fish genus *Pomolobus*) and concludes: ". . . the presence or absence of fertile hybrids is not a reliable species character", and, because the species concept is still quite unsettled, it "is basically a human concept."[20]

Many geneticists would define a species as the ability to interbreed freely. Theodosius Dobzhansky, for example, separates into different species two strains of fruit flies which are structurally identical in the female and practically so in the male, largely because of a chromosomal defect in one which prevents easy hybridization and male fertility.[21] Others such as Bullock feel that the concept of species must also include structural identity; Bullock gives pointed examples to sustain this position.[22]

Smugness, of course, is unpleasant wherever it is found. It is especially so among professing Christians who absorb the theories of unbelievers and then tout their position as that of the majority. Consider the statement of J. Lawrence Kulp, professor of geology at Columbia University and director of the geochemistry laboratory at the Lamont Geological Observatory, Palisades, New York: "The concept that earth history has encompassed millions of years became established with the development of the geological sciences."[23] Such an uncritical assessment prevents objective evaluation. Professor Kulp was once a member of the nominally fundamentalist American Scientific Affiliation, where he consistently and

---

19. "Incipient Intraspecific-Isolating Mechanisms in *Rana pipiens,*" *Genetics,* 30 (1946), pp. 304-326. "Hybridization between *Rana palustres* and Different Geographical Forms of *Rana pipiens,*" *Proceedings of the National Academy of Science,* 32 (1946), pp. 209-212.
20. *Evolution and Christian Thought Today,* ed. Russell L. Mixter (Grand Rapids: Eerdmans, 1966), pp. 111-113.
21. *Heredity and the Nature of Man* (New York: Harcourt, Brace and World), pp. 84f.
22. *Evolution and Christian Thought Today,* p. 111.
23. "Geological Time Scale," *Science,* 133 (April 14, 1959), p. 1105.

uncritically espoused the evolutionary views popular among his coworkers in the field of geology.

Intolerance

While the evolutionist expects toleration of his teaching in public and often private institutions, he is intolerant of the concept of special creation. The horticulture professor in Nebraska, after his view of evolution was refuted, would not permit the government pickup to be used for church attendance. The graduate assistant who displayed a portrait of Albert Einstein above his desk finally said: "We teach evolution here at this university, and if you don't believe in evolution you shouldn't be here!" This belies the evolutionists' claims to favor freedom of speech and freedom of thought.

During my undergraduate years at Purdue University, I learned how their intolerance could affect a creationist's career. In my sophomore year, the professor of plant anatomy, an agnostic, asked me to work for him in my free hours. This would provide good experience as well as remuneration, and I was glad for the opportunity. The work involved preparing microscope slides for laboratory classes. The professor drilled me in the proper techniques of cutting, staining, and mounting the ultrathin plant sections. I thoroughly enjoyed the work, and the professor decided to recommend me for a scholarship in the botanical sciences to a friend of his at the University of California, where I could obtain the doctor's degree. I was not a Christian then, and this had a tremendous appeal.

All went well until I became a Christian and accepted the inspiration of the Scriptures. As Laban's inclination toward Jacob changed, so that his "countenance . . . was not toward him as before" (Gen. 31:2), the professor's attitude toward me almost completely reversed. Before, he had boasted that I was "better without a course in microtechnique than students with the course." But now he rationalized that I was more of the scholar type who was not as adept with the hands; on another occasion he downgraded my intelligence, inferring my grade average was high because I was a bookworm. I explained that I worked up to thirty hours per week apart from my studies and often had time to read over my lesson only once. He resolved, however, that he could no longer recommend me for the scholarship. This bombshell fell in my senior year (about one year after my conversion), when scholarships were scarce, and we were still feeling the effects of the depression of the thirties.

Fortunately, the head of the botany department knew the situation and wrote the professor in California. My overseer, under pressure from his superior, finally relented and recommended me for the scholarship, which the gracious California botanist offered. This vindicated me, but by that time I had already accepted an assistantship at the University of Michigan.

The Christian science student can almost expect intolerant opposition in his oral examination for the Ph.D. degree. This examination culminates a period of arduous study and research usually lasting seven or eight years, three or four of which are on the graduate level. His investment in time and money represents a sacrifice that is drawn out over years. His inquisitors can ask anything about his field, even about its historical development over the preceding century. It can be very subjective, and the prejudices of the examiners can influence considerably their questions and evaluation of the answers. Most examiners are fairly lenient, however, and seldom fail a candidate. The Christian must not only know his secular material as well as other candidates, but also must be prepared to defend his conviction that God created the universe, as the following examples demonstrate.

The first example was a candidate for the doctor's degree in zoology from the University of Michigan. When asked whether he believed in evolution, he replied in the negative. When asked to explain his view, he did the best he could. His examiners said they could not recommend anyone who put his own personal views above "the voice of the entire scientific world." This student was refused, not because he demonstrated inadequate preparation in his field, but because of his religious beliefs. Suffice it to say, the examination should test *knowledge and not beliefs*. In this case his *beliefs* about evolution were questioned, not his knowledge of his field of study or even his knowledge of evolution.

At the University of Virginia, a candidate for the doctor's degree in zoology replied in the negative when asked if he believed in evolution. When asked to defend his views, however, he warily refused. This irritated his examiners, but they gave him his degree anyway.

Both examples were related to me by nominally evangelical Christians who were critical of the candidates, in the first instance because the candidate had the audacity to *explain* his minority view and in the second because the candidate *refused* to explain it! These nominal Christians had compromised to get by their examiners. The first, when asked if he believed in evolution, weakly replied that he "didn't see how you could explain some things otherwise"; the second deftly avoided the question by saying, "According to Darwin . . ." and not committing himself.

Another example was a doctoral candidate in botany at Purdue University. He had been a foreign missionary in the South Seas and returned to the United States to become an instructor in biology. He had done his work well, had performed his duties as a laboratory assistant faithfully, and had completed all the requirements for the doctor's degree except the oral examination. I knew well the members of his examining committee. One was the head of the department, who had written in my defense to the University of California; another was professor of plant physiology, a rather likable and easygoing but hard-grading instructor; the third was the notorious professor in plant anatomy for whom I then worked. The oral examination proceeded smoothly while the first two professors questioned the candidate, and they intended to pass him. When the third professor had his turn, however, he wasted no time in demontrating his dislike for the candidate. The candidate's history of being on the foreign mission field was against him. The veteran agnostic fired one question after another at the man until he became confused and made some errors. The professor seized upon these and insisted that he could not pass such a man.

So the Christian who is a candidate for the doctor's degree may find his entire work on the graduate level destroyed, in the name of science, by an intolerant evolutionist. This helps to explain why there are not more outspoken Christians with advanced degrees in biological sciences.

A physician friend recently told about his interview with the admissions committee at the Indiana University Medical School. Three times he was asked how he would answer an examination question involving evolution. Each time he told them that he would say that it is only a theory. He was accepted, he felt, only through the grace of God.

We conclude, therefore, that the evolutionist pleads for freedom of expression when he is in the minority, but, when he is in the driver's seat, grants no freedom to his opposition.

Dishonesty

The public has been made to feel that the very nature of the scientist's training insures his honesty and integrity. When the white-cloaked scientist announces his most recent "findings," they are accepted as scientifically proven. One may question the honesty of statesmen, philanthropists, educators, and Christian ministers, but not of scientists.

This conception of the scientist's lofty character and devotion to the truth is more fiction than fact, for the scientist is of the same flesh and blood as everyone else and is equally susceptible to the deceitfulness of sin.

Some years ago, a noted scientist on the staff at the University of Michigan took his own life when it was discovered that he had fraudulently misused funds. Newsmen were mystified that a highly salaried professor would stoop to such larceny, especially of only $400. The professor evidently had beome so arrogant that he could rationalize that he was worth even more to the institution than he was paid. The student rarely chooses science for a life calling out of a desire to solve the ills of mankind, any more than youths choose farming to provide nutrition for the hungry. The one chooses science because he enjoys scientific endeavor, and the other decides to farm because he likes farm life, and both hope to make a good living. Ideals, particularly Christian ideals, rarely bear on the decision.

The physician who feels called to minister to the needs of suffering humanity has won probably more respect and affection than any other scientist. This was especially true when plagues and epidemics robbed him of his sleep for days on end, and when financial rewards were less than they are now. However, men of questionable ideals have chosen medicine, just as they have other professions. They are especially attracted to it as the financial remuneration for doctors continues to rise.

With the advent of Medicare, unprincipled and dishonest practices have come to light; some doctors misrepresent case reports in order to increase their revenue from Medicare patients. One aroused physician, writing in *Medical Economics,* expressed with alarm and concern his discovery that doctors are as prone to falsify as any other group: "What's happened is exactly what you might expect of plumbers, executives, bureaucrats — and doctors. I put them all in the same category because the inborn traits of human nature recognize no social or professional boundaries."[24]

In my observation of scientists, both medical and nonmedical, during seven years of graduate study, I found them no more honest than any other similar segment of the population.

Most scientists doubtless will object to this statement, believing that a certain halo surrounds their field and prevents them from sharing the depraved nature of those about them. They assume that the scientific method assures a love of truth and complete honesty.

This is not confirmed by experience. Despite the fact that we are teaching more science than ever before, students are not growing more honest. Rather, honesty, like other moral attributes, is declining in our culture, among students of science and graduate scientists as well as others.

We have already discussed the tampering with the bones of the now-discredited Piltdown man. Since most scientists have little acquaintance with facts of any given case, they must trust each other, and they can be easily misled. It follows that a few dishonest men in the profession can give a false impression of startling and indisputable scientific facts with evidence that is incomplete and even fraudulent.

A meteorite fragment containing carbon fell in southwestern France in 1864 and was reported to contain evidence of life from outer space. Not until 1962 was it given microscopic (and macroscopic) inspection. A French microbiologist found that the specimen had been altered by deeply inserting bits of gravel, coal, glue, and tissues and seeds of a common reed. The meteorite had fallen only five weeks after Louis Pasteur had delivered a spirited and "widely reported defense of divine creation as the only possible initiator of life"[25] The alteration was apparently a cowardly, underhanded attempt to discredit Pasteur's position by ridicule rather than evidence. But the hoax was not discovered for ninety-eight years.

Theodore H. Epp relates another interesting example.

His father was a missionary among the Hopi Indians in Arizona. One day another missionary read a sign along the road: "Dinosaur tracks — 100,000 years old." Upon investigation, he found in the

---

24. Luther E. Mastler, "We Doctors Will Be the Death of Private Practice," *Medical Economics* (February 16, 1970), p. 167. Used by permission.

25. "Faked Life from other Worlds," *Scientific American* (January, 1962), p. 52.

same rock the tracks of a large animal and tracks made by Indian moccasins. Then the missionary noticed that the sign was changed from time to time, and that each time the tracks became older, finally reaching five million years. Obviously, the scientists were guessing!

One day the missionary found some scientists there and asked them how long they thought man had been on the earth. They replied, "About 100,000 years."

The missionary then asked them to explain the moccasin tracks near the prehistoric animal tracks (which they had claimed to be five million years old) in the same rock. The scientists could not answer him. When the younger Epp later visited this site with the missionary, he found that "the scientists . . . had carefully taken a hammer and chisel and completely obliterated the tracks of the moccasins. They were completely dishonest."[26]

---

26. *True Science Agrees with Scripture,* p. 16.

13

Theistic Evolution

The church of Jesus Christ is a body of believers, transformed by His grace through the power of the Spirit and dedicated to the will and Word of God, even though this may expose the Christian to extreme peril. Each disciple of our Lord is a potential martyr, and in generations past thousands have advanced the borders of the kingdom by the boldness of their testimony, by their uncompromisingly sanctified lives, and by their witnessing of God to their fellow men through suffering and martyrdom. We should never forget the price of this faith in Christ that we now treasure. We should be able to say with the hymnist:

> O for a faith that will not shrink
> Tho' pressed by many a foe,
> That will not tremble on the brink
> Of any earthly woe.

Unfortunately, none of the martyrs' children can inherit their faith, and many of them do not choose it by their own free will. Those who love the world tend to gravitate to a position of compromise which, they think, allows them to be friends of the world system as well as of God. This, of course, is impossible, for the kingdom of our Lord and the kingdom of this world are at opposite poles. Any attempt to find a middle position is an abomination in the sight of God. This was the great sin of Balaam, who urged God's people to intermingle and find common purpose with the heathen around them (Num. 31:16). This tendency for compromise finds its expression in substituting feverish youth activities and social work for evangelism; political astuteness for spiritual warfare; militarism for martyrdom; and the fashions and ornaments of the world for godly simplicity. It is a nominal Christianity which says, "We can have the world and God too." Another expression of this philosophy is theistic evolution.

Theistic evolution is the teaching that plants, animals, and man gradually evolved from lower forms, but that God supervised the process. The theistic evolutionist is a nominal Christian who says, "I believe that evolution is a fact, but that God did it!"

How does this view gain a foothold? Put yourself in the place of an incoming freshman in a large university. The order of the day is change: a new rooming house, new classmates, new roommate, new subjects. Above all, the student is "on his own." If he has not been pressured to believe the evolutionist teaching in elementary or high school, he will be in college. It appears in one course after another, sometimes very subtly, sometimes rudely, but always with the assumption that it has been proven thoroughly by scientific research. He usually hears *nothing* to the contrary.

After awhile this daily indoctrination begins to make a dent. The student's head begins to swim in confusion. He does not share his budding doubts with his classmates or parents, for he is ashamed of his doubts. In his uncertainty he returns to the church which has helped to stabilize him in the past. Seemingly by coincidence a campus church nearby is holding a discussion on "science and religion" the very next Sunday, and Professor Jones of the botany department will be the main speaker. Since Professor Jones has spent a year in seminary, this could be a most interesting and helpful program. When the meeting begins, the student is there, and he is eager for the message. Professor Jones, however, says something about evolution being a fact that is now universally accepted because of scientific evidence that has been demonstrated by careful research. This, he says, only strengthens his faith in God, for he sees God as the sovereign Ruler over the world, the One who has fashioned it through the evolutionary process. We can harmonize science and religion if we see Genesis as a story which was never intended literally. (As a student in seminary, Professor Jones had lost his faith in Christ as our Redeemer from sin and in the Bible as the inspired Word of God.)

This disagrees with what the student had been taught in his youth, and he hopes that Pastor Smith of the local congregation, now rising to his feet, will clarify things and support the Scriptures as the Word of God. The minister begins with his usual warm, disarming smile: "I can most heartily agree with Dr. Jones' message. I see our Lord as a greater God for working through evolution instead of special creation. I find that agreement with evolution harmonizes well with my calling as a Christian minister."

Oh, no! Not Pastor Smith! He was always so interested in the welfare of youth. He would do anything for them. He appeared to be such a good example of the Christian life. And so our student finds himself gradually sinking beneath the waves of unbelief. If he had had better counsel, he might have stayed afloat. But the lack of proper counsel, coupled with one-sided teaching, has discouraged many from studying the matter more thoroughly. Let us see what light the Scriptures could have given the student.

Its Scriptural Refutation

The first chapter of Genesis and parts of the second chapter, which describe God's six days of creative activity and his seventh day of rest, require careful attention.

The First Day (1:1-5)

In the beginning God created the heaven and the earth (v. 1). This statement is undoubtedly one of the most majestic ever recorded. "In the beginning" — not the beginning of God, who obviously antedated this event, but the beginning of the earth, its atmosphere, the solar system, and all the starry hosts of the universe. They were created by God. The language is simple and unmistakable. The Hebrew word for heaven is the plural form. Some commentators such as James G. Murphy of Belfast have argued that it refers to all the heavenly bodies. Although this is possible, it is more likely the "plural of expanse" (used again in v. 2), which designates the broad arch or expanse of the sky visible to man.

And the earth was without form, and void (v. 2). Some writers, Murphy being one, have claimed that *was* should be translated *became*, corresponding with the theory that the world formed in verse 1 suffered a great cataclysm which destroyed its habitation and marred its form. However, this is not the ordinary and usual meaning of the word, and no translators, not even those of the Revised Standard Version, have translated it *became*. There is no reason to infer a great catastrophe between the first and second verses. Verse 2 follows verse 1 smoothly, beginning a discourse which describes the *details* of the creation which verse 1 states in broad, general terms. Surprisingly, the footnote in the second edition of the RSV concurs. It paraphrases Genesis 1:1, 2: "When God began to create the heaven and the earth, the earth was without form and void." This unites rather than separates the two verses.

"Without form and void" is often translated, "waste and void." It was *waste* in that it lacked structure and was somewhat chaotic, unfinished by form or design, like the random waves of sand along the seashore or in a sand dune. It was *void* in that it lacked plants, animals, or human inhabitants.

Waters again exhibits the "plural of expanse," designating not separate waters but a broad expanse of water. The presence of the Holy Spirit in creation is apparent.

And God said, Let there be light (v. 3). The Hebrew word for God, *Elohim,* is plural, but the verb is always singular for the God of the Hebrews. This is in contrast with the expression used for pagan "gods" in which the verb is plural. One Christian school of thought argues that the creation of all the heavenly bodies was described in verse 1, and that this expression merely describes the penetration by light rays of the dense canopy of clouds that had enveloped the earth. This, of course, is hypothetical and necessitates a canopy that was thick enough to produce total darkness. It also supposes that this canopy was then penetrated sufficiently to illumine the earth, but that it was not penetrated completely. While this is an interesting possibility, there is no clear evidence to prove it. It neither affirms nor refutes special creation, or evolution for that matter. Such a canopy was possible and would be consistent with Scripture. But it was not necessary, for God is able to separate light from darkness without the sun and moon; He is not bound by the natural forces He Himself has created. In fact, each of His miracles demonstrates this. The above view is held by many Bible believers and is not to be confused with theistic evolution.

And the evening and the morning were the first day (v. 5). Many have argued that the Hebrew word for *day* can be used for a period of time longer than twenty-four hours and that this day could have been thousands or even millions of years in duration; the interpretation of *day* must be determined by the context. The context, however, is the expression, "the evening and the morning," which was regularly used to designate a day of twenty-four hours. The Jewish day began at sundown and lasted until the following sundown, the evening coming first, the morning second. This method of reckoning the day was established by God Himself, who commanded that the Sabbath be kept "from even unto even" (Lev. 23:32).

The Second Day (1:6-8)

The firmament and the waters were separated. *Firmament* in this chapter means either the atmosphere (vv. 6, 7, 8, 9, and 20) or space (vv. 14f).

The Third Day (1:9-13)

The dry land and the seas were formed. Dry land, of course, is necessary for most large plants, and plants are necessary for animals. The herbs, grasses, and trees were each brought forth "after his kind," designating the permanence and unchangeable character of species.

The Fourth Day (1:14-19)

The heavenly bodies were brought forth. Theistic evolutionists and many more-orthodox Christians believe that the heavenly bodies were created in verse 1 (possibly millions of years earlier, according to their concept) and are now made clearly visible from the earth by the withdrawal of the canopy of clouds from the planet, possibly through condensation like rain or snow.

The attempt to harmonize the days of creation with the theories of modern scientists is the underlying cause for the insistence that these days must be long periods of time. Even Wilbur M. Smith, formerly dean of Moody Bible Institute, who argues strongly for the permanence of species, states: "First of all, we must dismiss from our mind any conception of a definite period of time, either for creation itself, or for the length of the so-called six creative days."[1]

Behind this fear of designating the days of creation as twenty-four-hour days is the fact that the stars are millions of light-years away; if the stars were not millions of years old, we could not even see them, let alone calculate their distances, for their light rays would not yet have reached us.

---

1. *Therefore Stand* (Boston: W. A. Wilde Co., 1945), p. 312.

This disregards God's supernatural character. He is above natural laws. When Elisha's ax head floated and when Christ walked on the water, the Lord temporarily suspended the laws of gravitation. When Moses saw the bush burn without being consumed and when the three Hebrews walked in the fiery furnace in Babylon without being injured, the laws governing rapid oxidation were openly overridden by the Almighty One who set these laws in order.

But if God is not limited by natural laws, neither is He limited by time. This was demonstrated when Korah and his followers rebelled against the authority of Moses and Aaron and, indirectly, against the Levites. It was demonstrated again when the Lord commanded Aaron and each prince of the Israelites to fashion a rod, apparently of wood. Every man's name was written on his rod, including Aaron's on the rod of Levi, that God might cause the rod of the tribe He had chosen to burst into blossom. Overnight, "the rod of Aaron for the house of Levi was budded, and brought forth buds, and bloomed blossoms, *and yielded almonds*" (Num. 17:8), a process that by all natural laws would have required many weeks. This transformation may have taken only an instant. It is therefore evident that, when our heavenly Father spoke the earth and heavens into existence by saying, "Let them be for lights in the firmament of the heavens," the radiant energy from the myriad glowing bodies in space traveled to the farthest regions of the most distant galaxies, not at the rate of 186,000 miles per second (the often quoted speed of light) but in an instant, a moment of time.

The Fifth Day (1:20-23)

Marine and aquatic life and birds were created. The term translated *great whales* does not specifically designate the whale; it means large marine animals. However, the large whales far exceed in size any other creature, extinct or living, so they must at least be included. The evolutionist assumes that mammals developed on dry land and that marine mammals like the whale, porpoise, and manatee returned to the sea; the Bible lists them among the first animals to appear on the earth. Evolutionists also commonly believe birds to have evolved from terrestrial reptiles; the Bible puts their creation before that of land animals. Wilbur M. Smith attempts to harmonize these discrepancies:

> One should recall how closely related birds and fishes are, in structural matters. Both are egg-shaped, with gradually tapering

bodies for swift movement. As a rule, their main means of locomotion are not feet but fins and wings. Both are covered with
shingle-like fins or feathers; both have hollow, light bones; both
are egg-laying; in both the blood corpuscles are oval, not round;
and both possess a migratory instinct.[2]

While at first reading this statement is impressive, it ignores many
fundamental differences. The fish has a two-chambered heart,
whereas the bird has a four-chambered heart. The brain of a bird
is vastly more complex than that of a fish. In some cases the legs
of birds are well designed for rapid locomotion; the ostrich is able
to run sixty miles per hour, faster than the fastest Arabian horse,
and a kick from its powerful legs can disable a man or even a
horse. Finally, the pectoral and pelvic fins of fish corresponding to
the birds' wings and legs, respectively, are ordinarily used not for
locomotion but for balance, most of the locomotion being provided
by the caudal fin and the tail. The body shapes and egg-laying
properties are shared also with reptiles and amphibia. The modern
scientist would almost certainly smile at Smith's statement, as the
former feels he has "known" for some time that the birds descended
from reptiles. The scales on birds' legs supposedly betray their
reptilian ancestry.[3]

The Sixth Day (1:24-31)

Land animals and man were created. Increasingly, fundamentalists are trying to reconcile the Bible with the view of the majority of scientists. This does not demonstrate open-mindedness so
much as it does conformity to the world and a desire to court its
favor. While it may be true that men of Wilbur M. Smith's stature
are sincere in their desire to win respectability for the gospel by
conforming to philosophy reportedly based on science, they are
attempting an impossible compromise that will be ultimately fatal
to their cause. Smith's attempt to see a parallel between Genesis
1:11-13 and the Devonian period; between Genesis 1:20-23 and the
end of the Paleozoic era; and between Genesis 1:24, 25 and the later
Mesozoic period and early Cenozoic period treads incautiously on
the quicksands of a theoretical structure which, as we have already
seen, is based on the assumption that evolution is true. Three types

2. *Therefore Stand*, p. 323.
3. No evidence supports this claim. Marshall has stated: "The origin of birds
is largely a matter of deduction. There is no fossil of the stages through which
the remarkable change from reptile to bird was achieved." *Biology and the Comparative Physiology of Birds* (New York: Academic Press), p. 1.

of land animals are mentioned: *cattle,* which seem to be large, four-footed beasts; *creeping things,* (Hebrew, *remes*) which apparently are "reptiles and other rapidly moving animals" *(Strong's Concordance)* ; and *beasts of the earth,* which likely are wild creatures of the wilderness (it is certainly a general term). Where do the land insects belong in this list? It is unlikely that they would be omitted. First, they are of great economic importance. On the positive side, they are responsible for most of the pollination of orchard fruits, wild fruits, and many field and truck crops. They are of vast importance in this role. Large quantities of honey and beeswax are produced annually by bees. On the negative side, destructive insects feed upon man's crops and compete with him for food far more successfully than any other group of animals. In addition they parasitize his livestock, cause serious bites and stings, and carry many important and even fatal diseases. Second, they are numerically the largest group of animals by far. They belong to the phylum Arthropoda, which comprises three-fourths of all living animal species, most of which are insects (the spiders, millipedes, centipedes, and crustaceans constitute a small minority). Therefore, it is likely that the insects are included among the *creeping things.* The terrestrial worms possibly belong here also, though this is less certain.

The theistic evolutionist teaches that the Bible's days of creation parallel the steps involved in organic evolution, and that the Bible therefore supports evolution. The two are compared in figure 36. Each intersection of lines is evidence that the two systems are not parallel and, therefore, that the Bible does not teach any kind of evolution, theistic or otherwise.

God created man in His own image (v. 27). Thus man was created apart and distinct from all other creatures, exercising dominion over all other species from the very beginning. This cannot be reconciled with any concept of evolution, which of necessity argues that man is but a step above a slightly inferior creature.

The writer has met fundamentalists who concede that plants and lower animals may have evolved, but insist that man was specially created. This position is very vulnerable and inconsistent for several reasons. Most important, the Scriptures make no such distinction between the creation of plants, lower animals, and man. Likewise the scientific evidence, including the fossil record, offers no support. Therefore they are withdrawing to the last ramparts needlessly, evidencing more faintheartedness than open mindedness.

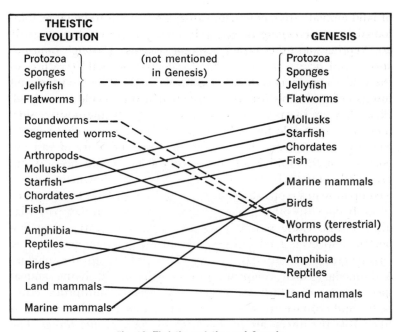

Fig. 36. Theistic evolution and Genesis

If the lower levels of plants and animals evolved, so did man; the failure of these fundamentalists to draw this logical conclusion suggests religious bias, which impresses neither their agnostic co-scientists nor their brethren who hold to the biblical account.

Let us make man (v. 26). The plural form has traditionally been cited as evidence for creation by the triune God. Recently, with the advent of modern theology, this view has waned in popularity. But verse 2 refers to the Spirit's presence at creation, and Christ's presence is stated simply and forcefully in the New Testament:

> In the beginning was the Word, and the Word was with God, and the Word was God. The same was in the beginning with God. All things were made by him; and without him was not anything made that was made. [John 1:1-3]
>
> For by him were all things created, that are in heaven, and that are in earth, visible and invisible, whether they be thrones, or dominions, principalities, or powers: all things were created by him. [Col. 1:16]

And behold, it was very good (v. 31). In the gleaming pearls in the spider's web on a dewy morning; in the mirrored crystal waters of a mountain stream; in the breathless color of a lady's slipper, fringed gentian, and cardinal flower; in the sparkle and pristine purity of new-fallen snow under a full moon; in the plummeting swoop of the night hawk on a summer evening; in the glittering starry hosts of the heavens; in the radiant fire of autumn leaves; in the innocent eyes of a little child; we sense an echo that God's handiwork is still, even after the fall of man, very good indeed. How wonderful it must have been before it was marred by man's carelessness and greed.

The Seventh Day (2:2, 3)

God rested on the seventh day (v. 2).

This, like the phrase, "the evening and the morning," proves that the days of creation were twenty-four hours long. "God blessed the seventh day and sanctified it [that is, sanctified the day]: because that in it [this seventh *day*] he had rested from all his work which God created and made." If this seventh day were an era, He would have sanctified an era rather than a twenty-four-hour day. But He did not.

> But the seventh day is the sabbath of the Lord thy God . . .
> For in six days the Lord made heaven and earth, the sea, and all that in them is, and rested the seventh day. Wherefore the Lord blessed the sabbath day, and hallowed it. [Exod. 20:10a, 11]

The same Hebrew word for *day* is used in Exodus 20 and in Genesis 2:2, in keeping with the view that it expresses the same unit of time in both instances. If the days of creation were long periods of time, perhaps thousands of years, it would follow that God rested for an equally long period. Does the theistic evolutionist mean to say this, or has he simply not considered this point? Some have said that God did rest from creation a long period of time and that He still is resting. But, if He is, then no new species have been created and theistic evolution is impossible.

The Scriptures, of course, indicate that God did not create new species after the seventh day, and with this we agree. As far as "resting" otherwise, however, God has not. Soon after the creation "unto Adam also and to his wife did the Lord God make coats of skins and clothed them" (Gen. 3:21). In the New Testament, Christ attributed His ministry to the Father's working: ". . . but the Father that dwelleth in me, he doeth the works" (John 14:10); and again we read, "My Father worketh hitherto, and I work" (John 5:17).

The Sixth Day Reviewed (2:7, 21-24)

The creation of man was described in a general sense in Genesis 1:26, 27; in 2:7 some of the details are given. "The Lord God formed man of the dust of the ground, and breathed into his nostrils the breath of life; and man became a living soul."

It is again evident that man was created to be distinct and apart from all other creatures. He was *not* created from a lower creature which was almost like man, nor did God choose a certain stage of evolution and implant within it an immortal spirit and a consciousness of God. Man was made from the *dust of the ground.* Many will complain that we are too literal here. But there is not the slightest suggestion that this passage is figurative. It is a simple *history* of man's beginning, not an allegory on which we are to place a studied interpretation. Nowhere in the rest of the Bible is the creation account interpreted allegorically. Nor have we ever heard of what the theistic evolutionist considers *dust* to be a figure; he attempts to ignore it altogether.

All the beasts of the field and fowls of the air were brought to Adam to be named. Note that *none* of them very closely resembled Adam: ". . . for Adam there was not found an help meet for him."

You will remember from an earlier chapter that the best evidence we have indicates no appreciable changes in any species over the centuries. The lotus flower that sprouted from seed found in an ancient oriental canoe was exactly like the modern lotus in Japan, unchanged in many centuries. The mummies of Egyptians are identical to modern Egyptians, no progression being found in five thousand years (fig. 37). The deepest fossil-bearing rocks in the Grand Canyon have very complex arthopods, essentially indistinguishable from modern-day forms. For this reason the evolutionist is constantly driven to conclude that any changes must have required millions of years. Certainly, if changes were this slow and Adam developed from a lower animal, the differences in one generation would be imperceptible, and his immediate ancestor would have to be almost like him. But the Bible says clearly that there was none like this that could be his helpmeet, so God brought forth his female companion in a separate act of creation. If words mean anything at all, we must conclude that this is the message of Genesis 2:21-24.

We conclude, therefore, that evolution — even theistic evolution

Fig. 37. When Egyptian mummies, which are approximately five millennia old, are compared with their modern descendants, no evidence of evolution is discernible. If anything, the ancient stock is physically superior. (Courtesy of Field Museum of Natural History.)

— is neither scientific nor scriptural and that, even from the standpoint of logic, it fails to survive careful examination.

If there is such a strong case against evolution, why are so many ministers entangled with it? This is not difficult to understand. The seminary professor in many cases has a surprisingly inadequate knowledge of Genesis and in other cases has little faith in its inspiration. Also, he seldom has more than a smattering of training in science, so he looks to the scientist for the correct answers, confident that the scientist stands on impregnable ground, fortified with facts proven by carefully conducted experiments. He is most impressionable, therefore, and an easy mark for false teaching, reaching out for each new theory to keep abreast of the times. He then passes these theories on to his students.

A seminary student whom I met was a striking example of this. "Is it not true," he asked, "that the antlers of the Irish elk, for example, became progressively larger through evolution, so that finally they became entangled in the boughs of trees, and wolves and other natural enemies easily slew them?" I answered that, according to natural selection, only the fittest survive, making it impossible for any structure of an organism to develop beyond its optimal size. An elk with overly large antlers would die off by competition with normal ones. Thus, natural selection resists evolutionary change and substantiates the teaching of the Scriptures that species are constant. This was apparently an entirely new thought to him, and a good-natured grin spread over his face as he realized he had been an easy mark for a teaching that was untenable.

Students often lose their faith while studying in the seminary. At the University of Michigan, I met a student who had changed to engineering. He claimed that he had found "too many contradictions" in the Bible. "Is that so?" I asked. "Perhaps you would like to show me some." "Well," he said, "in one place the Bible says that Christ was born in Nazareth, and in another place at Bethlehem." I asked him to show me where the Bible says that Jesus was born in Nazareth, but he did not know. Of course, the Bible informs us that Jesus was born in Bethlehem and later was reared in Nazareth. I urged him to show me another "contradiction." He said the Bible states that Christ was declared to be the Son of God by His baptism in Matthew 3:17, by His transfiguration in Matthew 17:5, and by His resurrection in Romans 1:4. I was amazed that he considered these contradictory. "Let us suppose that we take this piece of wood and analyze it by flame tests, precipitation tests, and by X-rays which reveal the pattern of the atoms in the substances making up the wood. In each case we find that the element calcium is present. Do these tests contradict each other, or do they comprise a three-fold affirmation of the presence of the element?" He paused, reflected, and then admitted, "You have a point there." I asked him then, incredulously, "Is this the calibre of teaching in seminary that caused you to lose your faith?" He admitted with some embarrassment that it was. I invited him to come to church with me the following Sunday, and he promised he would. But each Sunday morning he found some excuse not to come; it became evident that his difficulties were spiritual rather than intellectual or scientific, and so I have found repeatedly among agnostics.

Its Practical Failure

The theistic evolutionist has argued that, by taking a more conciliatory and "reasonable" approach toward evolution, he can gain more respect from the unbelieving evolutionist and still not lose his own position in Christ. By any standards, this is wishful thinking and, indeed, a delusion! An increase in the teaching of evolution has been accompanied by an increase in disbelief in a personal God and in the blood of Christ as the atonement for sin. No recent studies have been made, but Dr. James H. Leuba found that, in 1914, 80 percent of incoming freshmen at College A were believers in God and in immortality (certainly minimal points in Christian faith), and that in 1933, after the teaching of evolution had become widespread in high schools, this had dropped to 42 percent.[4] The concept of theistic evolution has done nothing to abate this teaching of mechanistic evolution; in fact it is part of the same apostate movement, for many agnostic evolutionists, including Darwin himself, began as theistic evolutionists. The great majority of scientists, as Leuba showed, found they could not believe in both evolution and God; in this they were perhaps more consistent than their friends who espouse theistic evolution. At the same time, the effects of theistic evolution on a man are profound. His personal religious standards, his zeal for testifying for Christ as His Savior, and his belief in the absolutes of the Bible are all weakened. One who doubts the Genesis account will not be the same man he once was, for his attitude toward Holy Scrip-

---

4. James H. Leuba, *Harper's Magazine* (August, 1934).

ture has been eroded by false teaching. Genesis is repeatedly referred to in the New Testament, and it cannot be separated from the total Christian message.

Its Social Effects

The preaching of the saving gospel has a refining influence beyond the fellowship of the redeemed. The gospel has a way of so stirring the hearts of men that even the unbeliever has a respect for its precepts, and the community is a happier and safer place in which to live. Contrast this with the atmosphere in many Moslem countries, for example, where it is unsafe to be on the streets at night, or for women to be unattended even during the day.

The teaching of evolution likewise has a negative effect. When the Bible is attacked, even indirectly and subtly, it is felt in the very fibers of the fabric of our society. The evolutionist has not considered that, when faith in the Bible is taken away by false teaching, the platform of moral and social standards that have guided our youth in past generations is also removed. Without the Bible as a standard, each individual is left to his own discretion and is in reality plunged into a sea of unbelief without helm or compass. If he can no longer go to God's Word for his principles of right and wrong, where can he go?

At a church college alumni meeting, former graduates were given the opportunity to express their appreciation for the school and its influence on their lives. A physician from Detroit said with obvious tension that he appreciated the school "not for any dogmatic theology they taught" but for the principles of honesty and integrity that he had learned there. But the principles which he felt to be of value had come from the same Book from which came the dogmatic theology that he had rejected.

Similarly, a dentist who was an enthusiastic socialist was trying to impress a group of students with the glories of socialism and the failures of Christianity. After he had extolled the high ideals of socialism, however, someone reminded him that the principles of peace, concern for the poor, and compassion for the downtrodden that socialism claims to foster have all been borrowed from Christianity.

This is happening in many strata of our society. The smug college professor who teaches evolution through the week and sings in the church choir on Sunday may arrive at his office one Monday morning to find it occupied by student activists who are intent on getting from the administration what they demand. They are prepared to break the windows and furniture to do it. Bombs and burnings may follow. They seem to have no standards of right and wrong, and why should they? This same professor taught their parents a generation ago that informed people no longer believe the Bible, so they discarded the family altar of their forefathers and reared their children without it. This is also the basis for the violence that is breaking out in the cities over racial issues. When whole city blocks are going up in flames, it is time to consider what a generation without the Bible is like!

The end point of this rejection of the Bible is a return to the sordid level of paganism. A reviewer of an article on the unrest of today's youth concludes that "many seem convinced that total freedom from the dictates of authority would be an ideal existence. The real danger is that values of any kind may be losing their power, and that young people may find themselves in a valueless world. If that should happen our society may experience an unprecedented degree of chaos."[5]

Because of this lack of values, many young people are turning to occult movements which are moving into the vacuum created by unbelief in the Scriptures. Especially surprising is the growth of pagan witchcraft among the youth (and the not so young) of this generation.

> The practice of witchcraft is spreading in the U.S. In fact, the interest in witchery is so great that several high schools and colleges have offered courses in it — one taught by a witch high priest. At least 400 covens (witches' groups) now exist in this country, compared with 280 five years ago, and those in the Craft (as the witches call witchcraft) include celebrated actresses, Pentagon officials, Wall Street brokers, and Air Force officers.
>
> The modern witches emphasize that theirs is a return to the "Old Religion" — pre-Christian paganism — not to be confused with Satanism or the Black Mass or other mockeries of Christianity.[6] (Emphasis mine.)

Perhaps this should not be so surprising. Many modern writers have pointed out the parallels between our society and pagan Rome: degraded art, music, and literature, the sports craze, nudity, the growth of occult movements, and the ominous spread of Com-

---

5. "The Dangers of a Valueless Society," *McNeil's* (May 15, 1969). A review of "Why They'd Rather Do Their Own Thing," by Seymor L. Halleck, *Think* (September-October, 1968).

6. "Witchcraft Turns Groovy," *McNeil's* (February 1, 1970).

munism. With the ship of the theistic evolutionists obviously sinking, we implore them to abandon it, once and for all, and man the life boats and strike for the harbor of certainty and truth that we find in God's Word.

The Foundation of God

We stand either with God and His teaching of creation, or we stand with the evolutionist in opposition to Him. The issues are sharply drawn; there can be no compromise. You are either a Christian or an evolutionist; you cannot be both. God wants prophets, not politicians; not diplomats, but soldiers in the spiritual sense:

> (For the weapons of our warfare are not carnal, but mighty through God to the pulling down of strongholds;) Casting down imaginations, and every high thing that exalteth itself against the knowledge of God, and bringing into captivity every thought to the obedience of Christ. [II Cor. 10:4, 5]
>
> For we wrestle not against flesh and blood, but against principalities, against powers, against the rulers of the darkness of this world, against spiritual wickedness in high places. Wherefore take unto you the whole armour of God, that ye may be able to withstand in the evil day, and having done all, to stand. [Eph. 6:12, 13]

In former days many outstanding scientists testified without embarrassment of their faith in God (fig. 38). Michael Faraday (1791-1867), discoverer of the principles on which electric dynamos and motors are constructed, was one of the brightest lights in the history of physics and chemistry in England. He was also a Christian minister, preaching alternate Sundays in a small church in London and making extensive use of Scripture. Professor Rudolph Virchow (1821-1902), renowned Prussian anatomist and anthropologist and "the father of human pathology," was a devout believer and a strong opponent of the theory of evolution. So was Carolus Linnaeus (1707-1778), the Swedish taxonomist whose system for classifying plants and animals is still followed today.

In any review of French contributions to the world of science, the name of Louis Pasteur (1822-1895) will probably appear at the head of the list. He will always be reckoned one of the greatest scientists the world has produced for his work in chemistry, medicine, and bacteriology. In a public refutation of spontaneous generation, he gave an impassioned and widely publicized defense of special creation. Also outstanding was Baron Cuvier (1769-1832),

LOUIS
PASTEUR

LOUIS
AGASSIZ

MICHAEL
FARADAY

HORACE
HOVEY

BARON
CUVIER

Fig. 38. Many renowned scientists, including these five, have been creationists instead of evolutionists. (Courtesy of Chicago Historical Society [Pasteur, Faraday, Agassiz], Brown Brothers [Cuvier], and Indiana State Library.)

founder of the sciences of comparative anatomy and palentology. He was always an unswerving defender of special creation and, with his vast background in natural history and his lucid presentation, was able to defeat the challenges of the evolutionists who faced him in private discussion and public debate, a fact which Simpson himself concedes.[7]

Louis Agassiz (1807-1873), the Swiss-born geologist and zoologist who became at Harvard University one of America's outstanding scientists, was a strong, tireless foe of Darwinian evolution. So superior was he in his field that, "with Agassiz on their side, American scientists were convinced that they could more than match the accomplishments of the Europeans."[8] Samuel F. B. Morse (1791-1872), inventor of the telegraph, made the first message sent over the wires, a quotation from Numbers 23:23, "What hath God wrought?" Horace C. Hovey (1832-1914), the outstanding American authority on caves, organized some twenty Sunday schools in Fountain County, Indiana, and served in the Christian ministry into his seventy-sixth year.[9] John Bartram (1699-1777), pioneer American botanist, developed the first botanical garden in America. His home in Philadelphia, where his fine collection of native plants remains, is one of the showplaces of the city. One can still read on a stone window casing the following testimony, which Bartram carefully chiseled with his own hands:

IT IS GOD ALONE ALMYTY LORD
THE HOLY ONE BY ME ADORED
JOHN BARTRAM 1770[10]

The spiritual climate in which we live is less receptive to such testimonies, since most scientists today erroneously assume that Christian zeal is incompatible with their calling. However, we have the same resources today in Christ and the Word of God that these men depended upon. In the annals of the history of the Christian church, God has used fearless men who would not compromise with the opposition, but who would testify of the truth

---

7. *Life of the Past* (New Haven: Yale University Press), p. 141.
8. "A Gallery of 19th Century Scientists," *Medical Tribune* (April 11, 1973), p. 25
9. William R. Halliday, "Indiana's Father of Speleology," *Outdoor Indiana* (January, 1972), p. 23.
10. Harold D. Eberlein, "Philadelphia Houses a Proud Past," *National Geographic Magazine* (August, 1960), pp. 161, 167.

in Christ regardless of the cost. God wants men today who could say with the apostle Paul, "I am not ashamed of the gospel of Christ: for it is the power of God unto salvation to everyone that believeth" (Rom. 1:16).

Such a faith will sustain us in the storms of life and make us a lighthouse to those who are groping to find the way home to God.

Part III

Technical Refutation
of Evolution

14

Radioactive Dating Methods

Radiocarbon

The radiocarbon method is a revolutionary and ingenious tool for dating ancient objects. It is based on the fact that the upper atmosphere is bombarded with billion-volt energy from cosmic rays which give off rapidly-moving, small particles called neutrons. These in turn collide with nitrogen atoms to form radioactive carbon (carbon 14). It is thought that there are about a trillion ordinary carbon atoms to every radioactive one in nature. This carbon 14 can form carbon dioxide along with normal carbon, and enter into the food-making process in green plants which, in turn, are ingested by animals. Thus, at death, both plants and animals contain some carbon 14 which then slowly converts back to nitrogen until, at its end point (estimated to be at about seventy thousand years), virtually none remains. Up until that time, the intensity reading of carbon 14 is used to give the age of the fossil remnant.

This assumes that: (1) the carbon 14 concentration in the carbon dioxide is constant; (2) the cosmic ray flux has remained unchanged; (3) the rate of decay of carbon atoms has remained unaltered; (4) the relative amount of carbon dioxide in the ocean and atmosphere have not changed; (5) biologic activity, or external processes, have not affected carbon 14 amounts; (6) no contamination with modern carbon has occurred. All assumptions are open to question.

When the method was first used and its shortcomings could not be assessed, it was heralded throughout the world much like an outstanding new drug, the side effects of which have not yet become apparent. It enjoyed a certain immunity for a time; history extends back only about five thousand years, leaving nothing that could be used as a check. With the passing of time, however, doubts about its reliability have increased.

Dr. E. A. Hoebel warned, for example: "Carbon 14 dating presents a number of technical problems, and its readings need to be used with care. It is also limited by the fact that it is reliably effective only up to 30,000 years."[1]

In his very first attempt to check this method with objects of known age, Dr. Willard Libby, the brilliant nuclear chemist who discovered the method, estimated the age of an acacia beam from an Egyptian tomb during the reign of King Djosec at about 2000 B.C., short of its actual age by seven hundred years.[2] This was disappointing even to Libby, for the probability of error increases geometrically as the age of the specimen increases.

Uneasiness about the method is expressed by Charles B. Hunt, former president of the American Geological Institute: "No one seriously proposes that all the determined dates are without error, but we do not know how many of them are in error — 25 percent? 50 percent? 75 percent? And we do not know which dates are in error, or by what amounts, or why."[3]

This growing uneasiness is due to several factors. If carbon 14 concentration in the carbon dioxide of the air has not remained constant, then skepticism about the accuracy of the method would be in order, as has been frankly admitted: "It would most certainly ruin some of our carefully developed methods of dating things from the past . . . If the level of Carbon 14 was less in the past . . . then our

---

1. *Anthropology, The Study of Man* (New York: McGraw-Hill, 1958), p. 118. Used with permission.

2. Lyman Briggs and Kenneth Weaver, "How Old Is It?" *National Geographic Magazine*, 114 (August, 1958).

3. "Radiocarbon Dating in the Light of Stratigraphy and Weathering Processes," *Scientific Monthly*, 81 (November, 1965), p. 240.

estimates of the time that has elapsed since the life of the organism will be too long."[4]

Significantly, recent investigations have demonstrated this very fact, that the carbon 14 cencentration has *not* remained at the same level.

It is well established that the ages obtained on assumption of constant, initial concentrations can differ by several hundreds of years from historical and dendrochronological dates for certain periods over the past 6000 years. H. E. Suess presented the latest determination of the fluctuation of radio-concentration over the earlier half of this period, as adduced from dendrochronologically dated growth ring of the California bristlecone pine (Pinus aristata) . . . The carbon-14 concentration increases rather steadily during this time . . . He [M. Stuiver] analyzed measurements of the rate of sedimentation in lakes widely separated geographically, for synchronous events. Such events could be due to past, worldwide climatic changes or to changes of concentration of radiocarbon, as reflected in the calculated dates. These results confirm the change in carbon-14 concentration that occurred before 2500 years ago . . . This result is at variance with other correlations such as the Swedish varves.[5]

The other assumptions have also been affected by variations that were not originally forseen. For example, the self-absorption of carbon 14 specimens varies with the thickness of the sample.[6]

Contamination of the sample by external sources, particularly in moist situations, can produce very large errors. Workers at Lamont Geological Laboratory and Washington University refer to the difficulty of assigning accurate radiocarbon ages to old carbonate samples: "Even 2 percent of modern carbon can give this sample its apparent radiocarbon age."[7]

A similar caution is given by Dr. Ernst Anteus, an American authority on varve chronology. He points out the necessity of distinguishing between the actual age of the specimen and the carbon 14 determination, as "laboratory analysis does not determine

4. *Science Year,* 1966 (Chicago: Field Enterprises), p. 193.

5. V. R. Switsur. "Radioactive Dating and Low Level Counting," *Science,* 157 (August 11, 1967), pp. 726-27.

6. Richard W. Hendler, "Self Absorption Correction for Carbon-14," *Science,* 130 (September 25, 1959), pp. 772-77.

7. Thurber, Brocker, Blanchard, and Potralz, "Uranium — Series Ages of Pacific Atoll Coral," *Science* (July 2, 1967).

whether the radioactive carbon is all original or is altered in still other ways besides by natural decay."[8]

Contamination in seepage areas, flood or glacial conditions can produce disproportionate variations and unreliable carbon 14 readings, the error of which greatly increases with the age of the specimen tested. "The most significant problem is that of biological alteration of materials in the soil. This effect grows more serious with greater age. To produce an error of 50 percent in the age of a 10,000-year old specimen would require the replacement of more than 25 percent of the carbon atoms. For a 40,000,000-year old sample, the figure is only 5 percent, while an error of 5000 years can be produced by about 1 percent of modern material."[9]

How great the dimension of error can become is shown by the following: "What bids to become a classic example of 'C-14 irresponsibility' is the 6000-year spread of 11 determinations for Jarne, a prehistoric village in northeastern Iraq, which, on the basis of all archaeological evidence, was not occupied for more than 500 consecutive years."[10]

Note that the highly refined science of archaeology is preferred to such coarse methods as radioactive dating. This is particularly significant since the findings of archaeology harmonize so well with the scriptural account throughout.

Most important, the great flood in the time of Noah may have greatly altered these readings. If a humid, cloud-like canopy surrounded the earth, the cosmic ray filtration would be much higher and the carbon 14 formation lower. Such a canopy has been postulated not only by many evangelical Christians, but also by many evolutionists in search of a way to explain fossils of tropical flora and fauna all over the earth — even near the poles — and the very dense vegetation from which thick coal seams found today were formed. One evolutionist, whose work I read for paleobotany class while a graduate student, conjectured that the canopy must have produced almost steady rain from dense clouds, the resulting darkness being overcome by constant lightning bolts that provided light sufficient for photosynthesis!

---

8. "Geological Tests of the Varve and Radiocarbon-Chronologies," *Journal of Geology* (March, 1957), p. 129. Quoted in *The Genesis Flood*, p. 373.

9. F. Johnson, J. R. Arnold and R. F. Flint, "Radio-carbon Dating," *Science*, 125 (February 8, 1957), p. 140.

10. Charles A. Reed, "Animal Domestication in the Prehistoric Near East," *Science* (December 11, 1959), p. 1630.

Because of the many factors that could alter the carbon 14 reading, and the fact that, while the evolutionist reasons in terms of millions of years, half of the radioactivity of carbon 14 is dissipated in just 5,568 years, the search for a more accurate method of dating ancient materials has continued. In the past few years, the place of honor accorded the carbon 14 method in the scientific literature has been passing to the newer, potassium-argon method.

Potassium-argon

Radioactive potassium breaks down very gradually into argon and calcium. Because its half-life is much longer than that of carbon 14, the discovery that the potassium and argon could be measured accurately met with an enthusiastic response from most geologists and paleontologists. However, quite serious errors have been found in this method, also. Statements qualifying its reliability, such as the following, should be somewhat disquieting to the enthusiast: "The potassium-argon age of the metal phase of Weekeeroo Station iron meteorite is about 10^{10} years . . . but distinctly disagrees with a strontium-rubidium age of 4.7 x 10^9 years."[11] The uniformitarian recognizes both decay rates as accurate as a clock, but one exceeds the other by more than twenty times.

Again, ". . . in this meteorite, we conclude that the potassium-argon dating technique as applied to iron meteorites [although this specimen contained potassium] gives unreliable results."[12]

Similarly inaccurate results are obtained from sedimentary rocks that contain fossils: "The presence of 'inherited argon' in the anorthoclase would lead to too high an age value by the K-A^2 method."[13]

What are possible causes of variation in results from this method? "The data indicate that the amount of excess radiogenic argon-40 is a direct function of both hydrostatic pressure and rate of cooling, and that many submarine basalts are not suitable for potassium-argon dating."[14] If hydrostatic pressure could alter

11. Rancitelli, Fisher, Funkhouser, and Schaeffer, "Potassium-argon Dating of Iron Meteorites," *Science,* 155 (February 24, 1967), p. 999.

12. Ibid., p. 1000.

13. Fleischer, Pria, Walker, and Leakey, "Fission Track Dating of Olduvai Gorge," *Science,* 148 (April 2, 1965), pp. 72-74.

14. G. B. Dalrymple and J. G. Moore, "Argon-40: Excess in Submarine Pillow Basalts from Kilauea Volcano, Hawaii," *Science,* 161 (September 13, 1968), pp. 1132-35.

the amount of argon gas retained in igneous formations, it could do the same in sedimentary deposits, where countless tons of pressure were manifest in the heavy, watery layers of sand, clay, and gravel, up to hundreds of feet in depth. This would account for the erroneously high dates for antiquity arrived at by the release of argon from the lower depths. How wild the results may be was demonstrated by Noble and Naughton: "Ages calculated from measurements of radiogenic argon and helium from three basalts erupted into the deep ocean from an active volcano (Kilauea) increase with sample depth up to 22 million years for lavas deduced to be recent. [These at the top of the same formation were dated at less than 200 years of age.] Caution is urged in applying dates from deep-ocean basalts in studies on ocean-floor spreading."[15] This means that the rock at the top of the lava flow is dated at 200 years whereas the bottom of the same flow is dated at 22 million years!

William Straus and Charles Hunt, professors of physical anthropology and geography, respectively, at Johns Hopkins University, while reviewing dates obtained from Olduvai Gorge in Tanganyika by Dr. and Mrs. L. S. B. Leakey, point out the many variables of this method: the more-ready escape of argon from feldspars than from biotites; the size of the minerals; erosion from older trash beds in the surrounding terrain; the presence of older glassy lavas embedded in younger constituents; the absorption by minerals of radiogenic argon, released by the weathering of nearby deposits and transported to a bed by ground water, vadose water, or the soil atmosphere. They conclude:

> Because some of the Olduvai Gorge dates are inconsistent, some must be inaccurate; they may all be. Until further tests determine which materials give dependable results, we do not know which dates are accurate. Until this is learned, the indicated ages must be taken **cum grane salis** [with a grain of salt].
> Until the contradictory dates and the existence and duration of the unconformities are resolved, the dates are of doubtful value in formulating hypotheses about the rates of evolution of man and his culture, rates of other vertebrate evolution and migration, rates of soil development, rates of accumulation of volcanic ash, and the persistence of ancient lakes. Whatever the hypothesis, it must be frankly admitted to be speculative. We heartily agree with the already quoted caution urged by von

---

15. C. S. Noble and J. J. Naughton, "Deep Ocean Basalts: Inert Gas Content and Uncertainties in Age Dating,"*Science*, 162 (October 11, 1968), pp. 165-66.

Koenigswald, Gentner, and Lippolt. The ages of **Zinjanthropus** and other hominid fossils from Olduvai Gorge thus are **sub judice** [still uncertain].[16]

Other Methods

It should be apparent that methods of radioactive dating other than carbon 14 and potassium-argon will be subject to much the same errors.

Concerning the radioactive thorium and uranium methods, respectively, it has been found that the thorium[230]-uranium[231] ages have considerable scatter, making calculation of the original uranium[234]:uranium[238] values questionable and probably invalid.[17] One cause is the alteration or contamination of the sample. With calcite samples, for example, there is reason to believe that "the system has been opened enough to disturb the normal relations between nuclides of the uranium series."[18] Obviously, as increasing amounts of nuclear wastes are discharged into water and soils, the results of all radioactive methods will be of decreased value.

The helium-uranium ratios have been plagued similarly with variables that decrease accuracy. F. P. Fanale and O. A. Schaeffer have shown that an exchange of uranium between the fossil and its environment can and does take place, for "in some instances exchange can be detected in measurement of $U^{234}:U^{238}$ ratios in the fossils."[19] Again, "In the discordant instances either method or both may be in error owing to uranium-isotope exchange."[20] Also, "Secondary addition of uranium appears to be the most serious potential problem in the method, especially for Pleistocene samples."[21]

If radioactive sources are located in interstitial sites, and consequently significant interchange of uranium transpires between the environment and shells, for example, "the age could not be accurately determined from the measured contents of helium and uranium." Again, "It is unlikely that an isolated age on a given shell would yield a reliable estimate of the fossil age."[22]

16. "The Age of Zinjanthropus," *Science*, 136 (April 27, 1962), pp. 293-95.
17. D. L. Thurber, W. S. Broeker, R. L. Blanchard, and H. A. Potratz, "Uranium Series Ages of Pacific Atoll Coral," *Science*, 149 (July 2, 1965), pp. 57f.
18. Ibid., p. 57.
19. "Helium-Uranium Ratios for Pleistocene and Tertiary Fossil Aragonites," *Science*, 149 (July 16, 1965), p. 312.
20. Ibid., p. 315.
21. Ibid., p. 316.
22. Ibid.

An unanticipated source of error is helium, which is present in living aquatic animals. "The most serious analytical limitation encountered was that modern samples, especially of coral, which should have contained virtually no helium, often yielded apparent helium contents."[23]

In reviewing radioactive methods, it is important to recall that the carbon 14 method, even apart from other considerations, has a half-life of little more than five thousand years: therefore, even its most enthuiastic supporters limit its efficacy to thirty thousand years, and others like Professor John N. Moore limit it to five thousand years. On the other hand, radioactive potassium has a half-life of 1.3 billion years, and its use for dating objects at less than one billion years becomes inaccurate in geometric proportion to its recency. Its measurements of fossil age must be considered far too coarse, much like measuring the length of bacteria with a yardstick. This is another important reason why the estimates of the ages of fossils placed at thousands and million of years are not to be taken seriously.

We therefore conclude that the evolutionist who employs radioactive dating methods stands on very uncertain and unproven ground.

Pleochroic Halos

Robert Gentry, a physics professor, recently investigated pleochroic halos, which as he indicates "provide the only means for studying the radio-active transformation of elements in the earth."[24] These halos, seen best in mica, are radiation-damaged regions surrounding tiny radioactive inclusions. Sometimes they contain uranium or thorium. They are spherically concentric shells that are colored. Under the microscope they appear merely as rings. Gentry has perfected a technique for producing clear microphotographs of these rings, which vary in color, size, number, character, and spacing, depending on the substance that produces them. He began his study to prove the constancy of radioactive emissions through the ages, in line with uniformitarian thought. If the rate of decay of the nucleus is constant, then the radioactivity in certain "D" halos should be extinct. However, he discovered and photographed "alpha-particles," a product of radioactivity still emanating from

---

23. Ibid., p. 312.
24. "Cosmology and Earth's Invisible Realm," *Medical Opinion and Review,* (October, 1967), p. 75.

the nucleus. Interestingly, no one had ever before performed an experiment to test the concept; it was simply assumed by the uniformitarian school.

Gentry concluded that the existence of polonium halos disproves the theory that the earth was formed by a hot gaseous mass, cooling and solidifying gradually over hundreds of millions of years: "If this were so, polonium halos could not possibly have formed because all the polonium would have decayed soon after it was synthesized [and thus disappeared from the earth's crust]."

Another of Gentry's conclusions is equally arresting. Inasmuch as some of the elements producing these halos have very short half-lives, some perhaps less than a second, and are not associated with a mother nucleus of a heavier radioactive element, they must have been created at almost precisely the same time as the rocks. He asks: "Is it conceivable that one of the oldest cosmological theories known to man is correct after all? Could the earth have been created by fiat?"[25] The reference to special creation is unmistakable.

A final conclusion of the greatest importance is given in Gentry's words: "In the meantime, my investigation of the uranium and thorium halos disclosed a startling circumstance: the radioactive decay rates had probably changed considerably during geological time." And again, "I will say only that a time discontinuity in the space time column has seemingly occured more than once."[26] These conclusions take a long, hard swing at the uniformitarian concept, and they do not miss.

25. Ibid., p. 78.
26. Ibid., p. 79.

15

Comparative Blood Tests

Years ago it was discovered that, if human serum was injected in increasing amounts into an animal like the rabbit, it would produce antibodies against the serum. After receiving large amounts of the human serum, the animal is killed and the blood drawn off. When the resulting antihuman serum is mixed with a solution of human serum, a heavy white precipitate is formed; when mixed with the serum of beasts, the precipitate is produced in smaller amounts. About 1902, the English evolutionist Nuttall pointed out that the precipitate was absent if reptiles were used rather than rabbits, present in small amounts if birds were used, present in greater amounts if hoofed animals were used, and fairly heavy if apes were used.

This is not surprising, for differences in complexity would be expected to be somewhat parallel in internal as well as external structures, and on the chemical and cellular levels as well as in gross anatomy. This is consistent with our beliefs that a sovereign Being created the universe in an orderly fashion and that similarities do not prove ancestral relationships. Further, other investigators have found that many animals do not fit into the sequence as expected.

More recently, this argument has been revived, using other proteins of the blood, with an accentuated dogmatism. In the University Explorer Broadcast (April 5, 1970) at the University of California, Hale Sparks announced that now scientists *know* how to identify evolutionary change by the number of similarities and differences in the blood proteins (hemoglobin, insulin, cytochromes, etc.) : "There's a kind of clock, now, that tells us when man first parted company with his fellow primates, the anthropoid apes. According to the clock, that happened some four to five million years ago."[1] If we were to find such a precise gradation, we would explain it by the fact that all things were created by the same Creator who has demonstrated order in His universe in many ways. However, it happens that this supposed gradation occasionally fails to fit the evolutionary scale.

Despite Sparks' confident air, which is reminiscent of the dogmatism of the proponents of the age and area theory a generation ago, the argument has many weaknesses. In the same issue of the *Journal of the American Scientific Affiliation,*[2] Duane T. Gish refutes it with the following facts:

(1) Its proponents deny their own theory of natural selection, because changes in protein structure were due to "neutral mutations," and they became fixed by "random genetic drift." "Neutral mutations," they say, have neither a detrimental nor a beneficial effect on the function of the organism." This they must say to bolster their position, since natural selection (which depends on *changes* in the environment) prevents a constant and regular rate of change in mutations.

(2) Measurements to establish activity of proteins as neutral mutations have been done *in vitro* (i.e., in the test tube, outside of the body) rather than in living cells. With such intracellular enzymes as cytochrome C, for example, the validity of such testing is particularly open to question.

(3) Human hemoglobin structure does not dovetail with the concept of neutral mutations in blood proteins; when one site of the chain of proteins has mutated, the usual result is anemia. The proteins are quite specific within each species, again not in accord with the concept of neutral mutation.

---

1. "The Protein Clock," *Journal of the American Scientific Affiliation* (December, 1971), pp. 123-128.
2. "An Inconsistent Position," *Journal of the American Scientific Affiliation* (December, 1971), pp. 125-27.

(4) Many features in the structure of proteins have been discovered which do not agree with the theory:

a) The insulins of the sperm whale and of the fin whale differ from that of the sei whale, but are identical with those of the dog and pig.

b) The insulin of the guinea pig does not closely resemble that of any other known insulin. Its protein structure differs in eighteen ways from both the rat's (a fellow rodent) and man's.

c) The structure of rattlesnake cytochromes varies in twenty-two places from those of the turtle, another reptile, and in only fourteen places from those of man.

d) Thomas Jukes and Richard Holmquist have bolstered Gish's argument. They compared the rattlesnake and turtle and found a difference of 21 amino acid residues per 100 condons, which is significantly larger than many differences between members of widely differing groups or classes: "For example, 17 between chicken and lamprey, or 16 between horse and dogfish, or even 15 between dog and screw-worm fly in two different phyla."[3]

Moreover, Sparks claims, "Now, much to the surprise of most evolutionary biologists, it's been found that the rates of incorporation of mutations into proteins seem to be nearly constant over evolutionary time."[4] This is a very important — in fact, necessary — element in Sparks' argument, but he offers no evidence for it. In fact, it is impossible to prove.

Professor Ralph W. G. Wyckoff of England recently analyzed proteins in animal fossils and published his results.[5] A reviewer of Wyckoff's book comments: "During the past decade, organic portions of fossil bones and shells have been analyzed to learn if and when these substances have undergone evolutionary changes. This is the principal concern of this book, and the major conclusion is reached that 'analyses made of the oldest fossils thus far studied do not suggest that their proteins were any simpler than those now being produced.' "[6] We see the case for the "evolutionary clock" fading as the evidence comes in.

---

3. "Evolutionary Clock: Non-Constancy of Rate in Different Species," *Science,* 177 (August 11, 1972).

4. Sparks, "The Protein Clock," p. 126.

5. *The Biochemistry of Animal Fossils* (Baltimore: Scientechnica).

6. Thomas J. M. Schopf, *Science,* 178 (December 8, 1972), p. 1086.

16

Creation-Evolutionism

Recently a body of nominally-fundamentalist scholars has argued that scientific evidence for change in species through the millenia of time is too great to deny. Largely spearheading the movement are two faculty members from Wheaton College, which had long been known for its militant fundamentalism. Russell L. Mixter, respected chairman of the zoology department, edited an influential volume entitled *Evolution and Christian Thought Today* (ECTT).[1] Cordelia Erdman Barber, former instructor in geology at Wheaton and an outspoken opponent of the old creationist school, wrote the chapter on fossils. James Oliver Buswell III, another contributor, teaches anthropology at Wheaton. Most of the thirteen contributors have earned the Ph.D. degree. This book has had widespread influence in fundamentalist circles, swinging many to its position from the orthodox creationist position. Christians of equal stature in scientific circles, however, dissent from the new teaching. Most of the contributors have been active in the American Scientific Affiliation, which began many years ago at Moody Bible Institute for the purposes of buttressing the position of special, divine creation and widening the testimony to it. Once advocates of creation-evolutionism gained control of the ASA, a

---

1. Grand Rapids: Eerdmans, 1959.

large delegation withdrew to form the Creation Research Society, which now has more than two thousand members, over five hundred of which possess advanced degrees.

The authors of ECTT are to be commended for enunciating their position with clarity. They argue that in the beginning God created the heavens and the earth, and all the species of plants and animals then existent; the larger groups of living things (i.e., phyla, classes, and orders) that exist today were created at that time; but in the interval the evolutionary process has been at work, so that *within each order,* the families, genera, and species are different than they were in the beginning. We have called this concept creation-evolutionism, as it credits God with creating all things in the beginning, but holds that evolution has developed different types in the meantime. This differs from the usual teaching of theistic evolution that all living things were originally derived from one living cell by divinely-guided evolutionary processes.

More recently, creation-evolutionism was expounded further in the December, 1971, issue of the *Journal of the American Scientific Affiliation.* I shall refer to some of these articles as well in this discussion.

Inconsistencies

As one begins to read ECTT, he is impressed with the consistency of its message: "the ancestors of the orders were created" (Mixter), and evolution developed new families, genera and species within the orders; it speculates that these ancestors may have been created centuries apart. (However, it must be remembered that these writers were selected because they shared this position, and that had thirteen scientists from the Creation Research Society written the chapters, an equal unanimity would have been manifest.) As one reads further, this apparent unanimity diminishes when Mixter revises his position on gaps in the fossil record, following Simpson by granting that "it might be necessary to assume that one order did evolve from another."[2] Buswell echoes this uncertainty, stating that in some cases everything under an entire phylum, such as classes and orders, may have evolved, but that "in the case of man, a much lower category, perhaps genus, would apply."[3] To the mechanistic evolutionist the latter statement will

---

2. Ibid., p. 183 (footnote).
3. Ibid., p. 183. (See also Henry on p. 208.)

simply reflect a theological bias foreign to an objective, scientific approach.

They are inconsistent in their attitude toward those with whom they disagree. Buswell, for example, quotes one mechanist after another to show the latter's intolerance and arrogance, yet he reveals a similar attitude toward his more conservative brethren: "Creationists, due to their own peculiar tradition of fending off the advances of science, have failed to formulate this alternative in a scientifically respectable manner."[4] By applying the term "scientific creationism" to his school of thought, he infers that those now in the Creation Research Society, for example, are less than true scientists.

Presuppositions

Presuppositions have figured into the positions of men on both sides of the controversy, and even those on the same side disagree on the role presuppositions should play. Barber says that the "basic philosophy of an individual will enter into his consideration of fossils."[5] Russell Mixter concurs "that one's attitude toward evolution depends a great deal on his educational and religious background . . . In plain English, there is much prejudice in this whole business of evaluating evolution."[6]

Hearn and Hendry state somewhat arbitrarily, however, that "scientific investigations must always be mechanistic in outlook,"[7] and that this is not contrary to a theological explanation of the origin of life. Cassel takes issue with this statement and questions their definition of *mechanistic,* saying that, "If this is so, no Christian can claim to use the scientific method because his 'frame of reference' is not mechanistic," and that "a Christian's assumptions or presuppositions must be Christian. There is no other approach to truth."[8] Morris and Whitcomb of the orthodox school agree: "Our conclusions must unavoidably be colored by our Biblical presuppositions."[9] When Cassel says that, where data are inconclusive, the Christian has as much right to interpret them in the light of Christian faith as the agnostic in the darkness of

4. Ibid., p. 184.
5. Ibid., p. 150.
6. "Developmentalism," *Journal of the American Scientific Affiliation* (December, 1971), p. 142. Used by permission.
7. ECTT, p. 69. Used by permission.
8. Ibid., p. 163.
9. *The Genesis Flood,* p. xxi.

his unbelief, he is absolutely right. And this is just the point: the *data* advanced for evolution are not conclusive.

Shall we conclude that the unbeliever cannot be convinced of special creation or that the Christian is a "special creationist" only because of his religious bias? Both of these opinions fall short of the truth. I became convinced of the fallacy of the dogma of evolution some time before my Christian conversion, through facts presented in Christian writings on the subject, and I personally know others who have done the same — some of whom have never yielded their lives to Christ. I cannot say that I had acquired a bias either way. Many scientific evidences point to a divine Creator, and many discredit the theory of evolution. The Word of God does the same, since truth in His creation will agree with truth in His Word. Here we need to distinguish between human reasoning and natural laws: the former is as unreliable as a quagmire for foundation; the latter are principles established in the beginning by God Himself, and will always be in harmony with His revealed truth. It is further true, however, that only the Christian can appreciate the creation in its fullness, as the handiwork of an omnipotent and loving God, and sense an overpowering inspiration in his innermost being, as he surveys the beauties of nature and sees God's hand at work, for *"through faith* we understand that the worlds were framed by the word of God . . ." (Heb. 11:3) .

Problems with Mechanisms

Again, the authors of ECTT have enunciated very clearly the evolutionary mechanisms that could lead to changes in species:

Speciation. Small, step-wise changes could occur in the species. There is great variation within some species, e.g., in the human species: in over-all size, body frame, facial proportions, hair texture, and in color of skin, eyes, and hair. These show evidence of many possible differences in alleles (similar genes governing the same part of the organism and appearing on the same point on the chromosome) . These could arise through changes in the gene, the additions of genes to a chromosome, the subtraction of the same during meiosis, different combinations of genes through segregation, independent assortment, and "crossing over" of chromosomes. Of these possible variations, some could be sorted out if animals were to migrate, or if great climatic changes occurred, and particularly if this were accompanied by isolation of some of the individuals from others of their species. Traits which were at a disadvantage in the old environment could then be advantageous to the species, and thus be sifted out and become dominating by the survival of the fittest in the new environment.

Phyletic evolution. This presupposes a closely graded series of transitional forms. Where these are supposedly found, the paleontologist infers gradual change in the larger group, from early (or simpler) forms to later (more complex) forms. The "evolution" of the horse is explained on this basis.

What do large gaps in the fossil record mean? The creation-evolutionist and mechanistic evolutionist disagree, the former arguing that such groups were independently created, and the latter that evolution took place by large leaps (quantum evolution).

It is almost idle to suggest that, while the phenomena mentioned under "speciation" certainly do exist as causes for variation, there is not the slightest evidence that these have resulted in new species. Such a conclusion, though using known facts, is still but a theoretical interpretation of those facts and cannot be considered proven. Further, as has often been pointed out, changes in the DNA that comprise the individual gene usually produce a mutation which, if it is not lethal, is almost always disadvantageous. It is also often inconsequential, as those mutations affecting flower color or, more rarely, bird songs.

I have not dealt at length with the subject of hybridization, because this adds no new genetic material or inherited traits, but simply reassorts characteristics that were already present, affording slight variations such as color and height (hybrid vigor does not, of course, alter the germ plasm). This is particularly so because normally the effect of these variations is minimized by the pool of overwhelming breeding stock that surrounds them, causing the original pattern of genes to prevail. "Inter-species" hybridization is common in some genera of plants, as in *Salix* (willows) and *Crataegus* (red haws), and in a few animals as *Canis* (dogs and wolves), but has demonstrated a tendency not toward greater complexity or a new, "higher" species, but toward intermediate forms. Experimental artificial hybridization, such as between bison and cattle and between radishes and cabbages, has no application in hybridization under wild conditions, where breeding between two like organisms is given exclusive preference.

As Robertson and Sinclair have so cogently argued, a detailed account of the mechanism of creation is neither necessary nor possible, as it is hidden in the mind of God, who has revealed in the

Scriptures all that we need to know of them. The number of such "explanations" that scientists have advanced testify to the fact that they can only be mere speculations.

The flora and fauna of Australia are considered the showpiece, or ultimate demonstration, of speciation and phyletic evolution, nurtured by superb isolation; we would do well to consider some facts to the contrary. It is assumed that marsupials, such as the kangaroo and koala, developed there because their peculiar structures and functions best matched the climate and other environmental factors.

However, of the mammalian species on the continent, only half are marsupials, and the others seem just as well suited to the environment. In fact, the dingo, a true placental canine, has tended to dominate many parts of the island. The evolutionist's explanation that the dingo was brought in by human immigrants some ten thousand years ago has no evidence to support it; no dingoes are found on the neighboring islands. Further, when other mammals are introduced, they seem to soon overrun the countryside, and this is only partly due to absence of their natural enemies. The European brown hare, brought into the country in 1859, soon overran the country and became such a pest, damaging huge tracts of grazing land, that state and national governments cooperated to destroy them. Even the dingo failed to control their numbers. The same species of hare, introduced into this country, has never flourished. These facts do not suggest that the Australian environment favors marsupial above placental development. Other native placentals include bats and many types of rodents. Mixter concludes that, since kangaroo fossils are not found outside Australia, it must not have been in the ark and the Genesis flood was local. This conclusion ignores the fact that conditions for fossil formation are rare and may not have existed after the flood along the route where the marsupials migrated to Australia.

Evolutionists since Darwin have asserted that marsupials developed in Australia, as animals differing from placentals, because of their isolation, and that this is the only area where marsupials have been found, with the sole exception being the opossum, which developed independently in North America.

The idea that marsupials are "almost entirely restricted to Australia"[10] does not take into account the existence of the water

10. Mixter, ECTT, p. 130.

opossum in Central America, and the many other species of opossum found in South America, whose ranges extend as far south as Patagonia and whose sizes vary down to that of mice. Fossil opossums have been found both in America and the continent of Europe. Some small species were found in the same western cretaceous deposits with beaked dinosaurs.[11]

Fossil kangaroo specimens, as *Macropus* and *Terragus,* have been found in Australia and for some time had not been found elsewhere, but this was due to insufficient exploration. Simpson had commented on the scarcity of marsupial fossils even in Australia, stating that "their fossil record is extremely poor, probably from lack of sufficient searching."[12] Now, however, it can be said that "kangaroos, now found only in Australia, once existed else-where too, for their fossils — one 12 feet long — have been discovered in Europe, and in North and South America."[13] This answers Mixter's objection.

South American fossils, however, exhibit many marsupials which "assumed the forms as well as habits of weasels, martens, foxes, wolves, and even saber-tooths [tigers]."[14] The latter were tiger-sized with a skull nine inches long. Of special interest is the wolf-like *Prothylacinus,* which appears nearly if not entirely identical to the present-day Tasmanian wolf (fig. 39) found on the island of Tasmania, just south of Australia. That the fossil *Prothylacinus* may well have been the same species as the modern Tasmanian wolf is revealed by the fact that the illustration of the former in *The Fossil Book* by Fenton and Fenton is obviously taken from the colored illustration of the latter in the *World Book Encyclopedia* for 1952!

How could this be? Wasn't Tasmania sufficiently isolated? Indeed one can ask where it would be more so. Did these develop independently, or did the Tasmanian wolf migrate to the island? Further, we may well ask if Dr. Mixter feels that the Tasmanian wolf was in the ark (since fossils of it are found elsewhere) and the kangaroo was not, or does belief in a local flood merely exclude the ark altogether?

---

11. Carroll Fenton and Mildred Fenton, *The Fossil Book* (New York: Doubleday, 1958), p. 379.

12. *Life of the Past* (New Haven: Yale University Press, 1953), p. 183.

13. Ivan T. Sanderson, "Migrating Mammals, Insects and Fish," *Marvels and Mysteries of Our Animal World* (Pleasantville, N.Y.: Readers Digest Association, 1965), p. 241.

14. Fenton and Fenton, *The Fossil Book,* p. 379.

Because of these facts, many scholars feel that the idea that marsupials developed in Australia has been exploded, and that they *migrated* to the Australian continent. Thus Fenton and Fenton conclude that "marsupials reached Australia in latest Cretaceous times, and entered South America before carnivores arrived."[15] James Beerbower concurs: "A marsupial population reached Australia at an early date."[16]

These scientists suggest that marsupials migrated southward from Asia along a land bridge, part of which is now covered with water. We observe that (1) many islands still exist which may have been part of the land bridge; (2) many Australian type species of marsupials, including twelve species of tree kangaroos (*Dendrolagos*) and the spiny anteater, a monotreme, are present on the neighboring island of New Guinea; (3) some Australian type marsupials such as the scrub wallabees (a type of kangaroo) persist on some of these islands, not only on New Guinea, but also on New Britain and New Hebrides (fourteen species of cuscus are also found on these islands, as well as two on the mainland) ; (4) many relatively shallow waters connect these islands. Thus, these species inhabit

15. Ibid., p. 379.
16. *Search for the Past* (Englewood Cliffs, N.J.: Prentice-Hall, 1960), p. 528.

Fig. 39. Evolutionists offer Australian animals as a good illustration of evolution, but fossils of the Tasmanian wolf (Tasmania being an island just south of Australia) have been discovered in South America. (Courtesy of American Museum of Natural History.)

portions of the land bridge between Asia and Australia which they reached before some of the connecting strands of land were submerged by the ocean; some actually reached the island continent. We conclude that Australian marsupials cannot be accounted for by isolation, for they were already of this type before they reached and distributed themselves over the Australian continent. The occurrence of so many diverse types of marsupials in the fossil record elsewhere, including some types now found living in Australia and its surrounding islands, bolsters this conclusion.

Wilbur Bullock concedes that without isolation a variant will tend to revert to the wild type. The examples he gives of change under conditions of isolation (the dark color phase of the nun moth, DDT-resistant flies, antibiotic resistant bacteria, and tassel-eared squirrels) are all examples of mere variation *within* the species.[17]

Strengths

These writers, opposed by both mechanistic and theistic evolutionists, have acquitted themselves well in showing the weaknesses of both positions, as well as the intolerance and dogmatism of many who advocate them. They have demonstrated strength in their refusal to compromise their convictions that God created all things that existed in the beginning, and that faith in Christ is the irreducible minimum in saving faith and in living the Christian life.

Carl Henry, discussing the confrontation between biblical theology and evolution, presents a lucid, overall view of the question, and perhaps stands on firmer ground than many other contributors to the volume. He reminds us that the vast majority of students have accepted evolution blindly.[18] He links the shallow, popular view of the theory, which considers man merely the most complex of the primates, with the gradual but certain turning away from the divine declaration that man was created in the image of God, and that man possesses a spiritual nature that can communicate with the Almighty. The theory has likewise led to a false concept of social evolution and progress (found in the "Polyanna" doctrines of the old modernistic theology) and to such monstrous philosophies as fascism and bolshevism.[19] Henry has been

17. ECTT, pp. 120f.
18. Ibid., p. 202.
19. Ibid., p. 218.

premature in his acceptance of speculation on the age of the earth and of creation-evolutionism. But his tendency elsewhere to insist on conclusive evidence, regardless of how widespread a teaching may be, is much appreciated, as is also his observation that the theory of evolution has been the most potent factor in the secularization of science.[20]

Disappointments

The creation-evolutionist may sincerely feel he has arrived at his position with an open mind, that he has been fairer with the facts than the older creationist school. Yet many will feel, just as sincerely, that his "open-mindedness" may be more accurately termed credulity. Buswell's statement that "an honest creationist will ask the paleontologist what he knows of the time of origin of animals, and draw his conclusions from the data,"[21] requires almost a child-like faith in the paleontologist. Buswell even admits the scientist must frequently change his position.[22] Any great dependence on the original interpretation would have been unmerited. Likewise, Dr. Mixter's attitude toward George G. Simpson borders on discipleship. At the ASA meeting at Harrisonburg, Virginia, he fervently stated, "I read everything he writes." While Dr. Simpson's writings are excellent in precision and organization, he cannot get away from a dogmatic stance that should make any objective scientist wince. For example: "Primates . . . arose from the insectivora, from which various early and primitive primates cannot be really clearly distinguished."[23] Again, "Amphibians arose from crossopterygian fishes in the late Devonian, from which almost perfectly transitional forms are known."[24] His drawing entitled "Restoration of Some Fossil Vertebrates," intended to prove the latter statement, is most unconvincing because of the large gap between the fishes and amphibians. The eusthenopteron, a crossopterygian fish pictured here is closely related to the coelacanth, which was formerly placed in such fossil series, but later was found to be very much in existence today!

Simpson's attempt to reinstate the discredited concept of inevitable social "progress" and justify the time and expense needed to

20. Ibid., pp. 217, 220, 221.
21. Ibid., p. 183.
22. Ibid., p. 131.
23. *Life of the Past,* p. 184.
24. Ibid., p. 179.

study paleontology[25] are likewise disappointing, particularly because our culture is not progressing but, "thanks" to such proponents of evolution as the paleontogolists, is rapidly returning to a frankly pagan state.

Most ominous is the end-point of Simpson's philosophy: "He [man] stands alone . . . with unique understanding and potentialities. These he *owes to no one but himself, and it is to himself that he is responsible.*"[26] Such seemingly atheistic statements should be adequate to remind us, even to warn us, that "the natural man receiveth not the things of the spirit of God: for they are foolishness unto him: neither can he know them, because they are spiritually discerned" (I Cor. 2:14). Again, "Blessed is the man that walketh not in the counsel of the ungodly" (Ps. 1:1a).

There are other examples of this overreadiness to believe the current popular doctrine. References to domesticated animals as evidence for evolutionary change are especially vulnerable, as are those' to the "evolution" of the horse from *Eohippus,* something which divides even the hard-core evolutionists.

A similar knowledge gap appears in the frequent assertions that similarity in structure argues for a common ancestor. It is strange that biologists have given so little thought to the periodic table of chemical elements, first discovered and arranged by the Russian scientist, Mendeleev. This is probably due to the modern tendency to know thoroughly only one's own specialty. The general chemistry student learns that the chemical elements, like the satellites of the sun, are magnificent examples of order. Most of the elements can be arranged in "families" or groups. For example, sodium and potassium and four other elements belong to one group of light "lye" metals which have very similar properties, despite different atomic weights, while calcium and magnesium and four other light metals belong to a different group in which all members are similar to each other, but different in many ways from the first group. These traits are governed by the number of electrons in the outer shell of the atom, yet they are not related in *origin,* for a radioactive member of the family, on degradation, does not ordinarily form another element of the same family. Here we see similarity of structure and properties but no common origin and evolution.

---

25. Ibid., p. 154.
26. Ibid., p. 155.

Most spokesmen for this movement seem to assume that the concept of catastrophism is no longer intellectually respectable. Is this true? Where and when has it ever been disproven? Disparaging remarks do not constitute scientific evidence, regardless of how often they are repeated. Cordelia Barber correctly states that organisms must be protected by "quick burial"[27] in order to form fossils, hence fossiliferous rocks are almost invariably sedimentary except for rare instances in which organisms were trapped by nearly-cooled lava. It is true that in a relatively few localities living creatures were entrapped in flowing resins or asphalt pools, and in more numerous instances in wind-blown loess. But the fact that the enveloping medium in the overwhelming number of cases has been *water-borne* sediment has been virtually ignored. Dr. Barber's reference to "the sedimentary clam living in an estuary and overwhelmed with mud during a spring flood" causes us to pause in wonder. Is this actually happening today? If so, where? Clams are not "sedentary" but possess a foot which enables them to crawl and dig, even in mud. How deep would the deposit need to be, and how fast would it need to be made in order to entrap the organism? I know of no relevant experiments, but it seems that the rate would have to far exceed that of a spring flood. She refers to fossil corals in sedimentary strata in Scotland which are distributed through a thickness of four thousand feet. Does Mrs. Barber really mean to say that these tremendous thicknesses of strata can be accounted for by ordinary spring floods? It is evident that countless tons of sediment suddenly covered these organisms, and that flood waters of tremendous proportions must have been involved. Further, her acceptance of the specimens from different levels as conclusive evidence of speciation and phyletic evolution ignores certain fundamental principles of scientific research: (1) The data must be carefully and critically reviewed in both the laboratory and the field by other scientists not involved in the original research. (2) Many more specimens are necessary for statistically valid conclusions. For example, in a family of four from two parents who are hybrid for eye color, although 75 percent of the offspring could be expected to have brown eyes, in any one family all children could be blue-eyed. (3) The many areas in which complex fossils are found in lower strata and the simpler ones in higher have not been taken into consideration in her conclusions.

---

27. ECTT, p. 136.

Lack of Nonconformity

It is easy to become blinded and lose one's objectivity when swept along with a spirit of conformity to the age. At a recent medical symposium that I attended, a well-known specialist in internal medicine who practiced and taught in a large medical school in Pennsylvania referred to a recent article on diabetes mellitis, which he considered the "most significant advance in our knowledge of the subject in many years." But, I was chagrined to learn the author's main thrust: man evolved from more primitive animals whose diets contained more protein, and man's diabetic problems stemmed from his inability to adjust to the increase in carbohydrates in his diet, now that he is omnivorous. This, of course, disagrees even with the evolutionist's concept of the survival of the fittest. The audience seemed to accept his conclusion at face value, despite the lack of genuine proof from experimental data.

Passive acceptance of current popular theories is attended by a loss of the individualism that is absolutely necessary for honest inquiry. As William B. Bean, M.D., editor of *Current Medical Digest,* has well observed: "The other powerful influence, and it affects academic medicine, too, is nothing less than the deadening of natural curiosity, the suppression of wonder, and the *security-minded acceptance* of authority that characterizes the attitudes of too many physicians who have come out of their medical school training with the *rigid stamp of the stereotype* ineradicably impressed upon them."[28] (Emphasis mine.)

The suspicion that the creation-evolutionist bears the stamp of indoctrination, that he has been stampeded to his conclusions not by the weight of proven *facts* but by the *opinions* of prominent authorities in their field, was recently heightened in the forementioned symposium entitled, "Creation and/or Evolution," published in the *Journal of the American Scientific Association.* Writers on both sides of the question appealed to authority rather than scientific evidence, making it obvious that this line of argument is most unreliable. They made statements like: "Along with the overwhelming majority of scientists, I believe . . ."[29] "All responsible anthropologists would deny this . . . there is a wide consensus of

---

28. "Opportunity for Research in General Practice," *Journal of the American Medical Association,* 154 (February, 1954).

29. Jerry D. Albert, "Scientific Tool or Creation Pitfall," p. 128.

opinion among anthropologists . . ."[30] ". . . the common opinion of the overwhelming majority of today's anthropologists . . ."[31] "[These] assumptions are unacceptable to the majority of anthropologists . . . I must rely upon those knowledgeable in genetics."[32] One author condemns another for "flatly rejecting the modern stance of several major scientists . . ."[33]

Those who have come to worship the sacred cow of "science," while attempting to retain their ties with the simple gospel of Christ, have compartmentalized their thinking, the very thing for which they condemn their more conservative creationist brethren. If they are going to follow the pied pipers who call the tunes in their respective fields of science, they can hardly criticize those who follow the pied pipers in liberal seminaries, which can also boast of the highest scholastic attainment. To assume that the theologian is less objective than the anthropologist, for example, is little short of naive.

This bowing before recognized authority has blunted the evangelical certainty and evangelistic fervor of the creation-evolutionist, by comparison with the creationist. Russell Mixter's lame defense of the moral values of the agnostic evolutionist is a disturbing case in point: "I think that Huxley, Dobzhansky and Simpson, as examples, would believe that moral wrong is any activity that impairs the full development of one's personality."[34] Such a nebulous "moral platform" is not essentially different from that of the modernist, or even from that of semipagan society.

Resistance to this spirit of conformity is necessary not only to the scientific endeavor, but also to the Christian life. The creation-evolutionist seems to wish to retreat from the biblical requirement of nonconformity. But the Christian must not be conformed to the world, not merely for the sake of being different or out of sheer stubbornness, but because the kingdom of light, in which he now takes his stand, is poles apart from that in which this present world is floundering in darkness and unbelief. He does not court opposition, but neither does he shrink from it, and he gladly confesses that we are "strangers and pilgrims" (I Peter 2:11). As one who has been rescued from the world of sin and transformed by the grace of

30. E. K. Pearce, "Proto-neolithic Adam and Recent Anthropology," pp. 130f.
31. Paul H. Seely, "Not a Viable Theory," p. 135.
32. Geo. J. Jennings, "Who was Adam?" pp. 137, 139.
33. Richard H. Bube, p. 156. Used by permission.
34. Russell Mixter, "Developmentalism?" p. 142.

Christ stemming from Calvary's cross, his ear is ever responsive to Him who exhorts us: "Present your bodies a living sacrifice, holy, acceptable unto God, which is your reasonable service. And *be not conformed* to this world: but be ye *transformed* by the renewing of your mind, that ye may prove what is that good, and acceptable, and perfect, will of God" (Rom. 12:1f.) .

Conclusion: The Christian's Focus

Some years ago I was preparing for a class in general science a demonstration of the fact that "white light" is actually a mixture of many wave-lengths and is thus many colors of light. It involved directing the light through a glass prism which would separate the rays. But the preparations were not going well. Although the source of light was bright, I could not throw the desired colors on the light wall. By placing a curved reflector behind the light bulb, however, I was able to focus the rays into a beam, and the resulting parallel rays of the beam, passing through the prism, cast the full spectrum of all the colors of the rainbow on the wall.

The Christian life, like that light bulb, requires focusing, and the Bible shows us how: "Finally, brethren, whatsoever things are true, whatsoever things are honest, whatsoever things are just, whatsoever things are pure, whatsoever things are lovely, whatsoever things are of good report; if there be any virtue, and if there be any praise, *think on these things*. Those things, which ye have both learned, and received, and heard, and seen in me, *do!* and the God of peace shall be with you" (Phil. 4:8f.).

A multitude of voices call for our attention, requiring us to focus on one of them. We who have believed in Christ and have been transformed by His saving grace through the blood of His cross, are not our own. We have been bought with a price, and are become living stones in the temple of the Holy Ghost (I Cor. 6:19f.). Our body and our spirit are God's, and our lives have become part of God's testimony here on earth.

When we experience regeneration by the Spirit of God, we are translated "into the kingdom of his dear Son" (Col. 1:13) and are become "partakers of the divine nature" (II Peter 1:4). Are you certain which kingdom you are in? Have you experienced the joys of a new life in Christ, in a new and glorious kingdom? If so, then you have likewise experienced an estrangement from this present evil world and are happy to be "not conformed" to it, for it is Satan's realm. We are not conformed to the world, but "conformed to the image of his Son" (Rom. 8:29).

We can perhaps better understand the importance of strong convictions and of a clear knowledge of God's purpose in our lives by considering the tragic groping of those who lack focus and direction. I have grouped them into four classes. The first two faced the apostle Paul at Mars Hill (Acts 17:16-18).

The emotional — The Epicureans sought "pleasure through experience." Seeking the transitory joys of this life in order to forget or ignore the painful and unpleasant, were hallmarks of this philosophy. Human nature has not changed since Paul's time, and we find the worldling, in his constant pursuit of satisfaction through new and exciting experiences, following in the Epicureans' steps. One also finds their counterparts among certain religious groups which major in shallow emotionalism and religious thrills.

The intellectual — The Stoics were at the opposite extreme. They were the hardened intellectuals, confident that through reason they could find their proper place in Nature and solve the problems they met in this life. They faced in the apostle Paul, however, one who knew that ". . . the wisdom of this world is foolishness with God" (I Cor. 3:19). Even Nicodemus, though a master teacher in Israel, needed to be taught the most important lesson of all, how to enter the kingdom of God through the new birth (John 3:3).

The activist — It is the activist who says, "Let's do something!" or, "We ought to give the young people something to do!" It's as if activity in itself has the blessing of God. The feverish activity of many charitable groups may be quite apart from God's will and program, and even the church activity of the vast numbers of nominal Christians may not stand in the day of judgment. Jesus declared: "Many will say to me in that day, Lord, Lord, have we not prophesied in thy name? . . . and in thy name done many wonderful works? And then will I profess unto them, I never knew you: depart from me, ye that work iniquity" (Matt. 7:22f.; see also I Cor. 13:3). The enemy of our souls does not care how religious we are or how active we are, so long as we are active in ways that the Lord cannot truly bless. How misguided such activity can be is shown by Paul's confession that his "zeal for God" before conversion had actually been working against God's program (Phil. 3:6).

The negligent — Quite in contrast with activism — and equally serious — is the failure to appropriate the grace of God in our lives, and to continue to use it to His glory. Jesus said that He is the vine and we are the branches, and added: "He that abideth in me, and I in Him, the same bringeth forth much fruit: for without me ye can do nothing. If a man abide not in me, he is cast forth as a branch, and is withered; and men gather them, and cast them into the fire, and they are burned" (John 15:5f.).

The true believer should shun the aimless and ill-conceived program of the activist, but he should be the most active of all men, directing his energies into channels that are firmly grounded in the Word of God and that alleviate both physical and spiritual need.

The voices of the world system under the direction of the Adversary are all around us. The Christian must be alert and conscious of the fact that he must walk a straight path of truth, even though the majority of friends and acquaintances may be falling off along the sides into error, compromise, and unbelief. As the voices of the "leading authorities" are mobilized against his position in Christ Jesus, he must learn to distrust them all (Isa. 2:22; Jer. 17:5-9; Ps. 1:1; I Cor. 1:21) and trust the one voice that can save him and lead him home at last when the twilight of life falls around him. In the classroom in high school and college, for example, teachers may attack the creation account as ancient folklore, and the moral and ethical teachings of Jesus as narrow prudery. But the faithful believer will remember that all such instructors, regardless of the excellence of their secular training, speak from the abyss of darkness whenever they sound off on any Bible teaching. We should be extremely wary of exposing our children to any form of agnostic teaching, whether in a state-supported or church school, for ". . . the natural man receiveth not the things of the

Spirit of God: for they are foolishness unto him: neither can he know them, because they are spiritually discerned" (I Cor. 2:14).

It becomes part of our Christian task, therefore, to continually sift and eliminate from our lives those elements that do not accord with God's Word of truth. As our perception of the eternal increases, our interest in the earthly becomes less and less and our curiosity about the carnal world about us strangely dims. The unregenerate mind shapes the news and fashions it according to its own base motives. Newsmen of radio, newspaper, and TV appeal to the base nature by way of nationalism, suggestive jokes, and indecent display of the body. In the religious field they favor the dead apostate churches, of which most are members if they are members of any.

Many of us would deny any interest in worldly culture; yet we may be more involved in it than we are aware. We are easily tempted, for example, to admire the person with secular talents. How often is it said, "Here is a man that is talented; we must use him!" Yet he might lag far behind others in spiritual gifts and steadfastness. And thus the Sunday school becomes dominated by the weakest members in the body; the superintendent may be a good speaker and the chorister a good musician, but they may not possess the spiritual depth or experience worthy of leadership (or even membership).

Culture is an artistic presentation of the philosophy of the unregenerate world. In the arts, for example, the measure of excellence is the degree to which one can skillfully change moods and provoke emotions. But the emotions range from the beastly to the divine, so the Christian cannot adopt the cultural view; he must be *selective* in the Christian life. We are to think on those things that will draw us unto Him who created us for His glory (Phil. 4:8f.), and to exercise ourselves unto godliness (I Tim. 4:7).

One example of the secular culture is the outstanding philosopher and distinguished Irish playwright, the late George Bernard Shaw. One of the most quoted men of our generation, his intellect was as sharp as a knife and remained so even past his ninetieth year. His analyses of the secular world were penetrating and more often caustic than not, but he perished in the darkness of agnosticism.

Or consider a famous Shakespearean actor. He took the part of Shylock in the *Merchant of Venice*. According to the script, he had loaned the hero, Antonio, a sum of money. If Antonio did not pay back the loan within a prescribed length of time, he was to pay a pound of flesh. When the deadline arrived and Antonio was not able to pay, Shylock demanded his pound of flesh; the decision as to where the flesh came from was his, and he demanded it come from the heart! So skillfully did the actor develop the vicious character of Shylock — so real did he seem to his audience — that the audience actually hissed. Yet at the curtain call the audience gave the actor a tremendous ovation and called him back again and again. How revealing! It mattered not *which* emotions were stirred but how *skillfully*. But we are reminded in Galatians 5 that the disciple of Chirst is to turn from these base works of the flesh to the Holy Spirit of God, that he may bear fruit that is true and eternal. For this reason Paul prays on the Ephesians' behalf that "the God of our Lord Jesus Christ, the Father of glory, may give you the spirit of wisdom and revelation in the knowledge of him" (Eph. 1:15-17) .

There is a focus in the Christian life, and that focus is on Jesus Christ. "And this is his commandment, that we should believe on the name of his Son Jesus Christ, and love one another, as he gave us commandment" (I John 3:23) .

May our own hearts and minds be so centered on the Word of the Lord that our lives may be as crystalline lenses, focusing the attention of those around us on the risen Christ, the hope of this life and that which is to come.

Index